THINE IS THE KINGDOM

THINE IS THE KINGDOM

The Reign Of God In Today's World

GENE MIMS

LifeWay Press
Nashville, Tennessee

5420-98

ISBN 0-7673-3015-3

Dewey Decimal Classification Number: 231.72

Subject Heading: BAPTIST DOCTRINE \ KINGDOM OF GOD

This book is the text for course CG-0368 in the subject area Baptist Doctrine
in the Christian Growth Study Plan.

Unless otherwise noted, Scripture quotations are from the *New American Standard Bible.* © The
Lockman Foundation, 1960, 1962, 1963, 1968, 1971, 1972, 1973, 1975, 1977. Used by permission.

Printed in the United States of America

LifeWay Press
127 Ninth Avenue, North
Nashville, Tennessee 37234

Contents

The Author

The author of *Thine Is the Kingdom: The Reign of God in Today's World* is Gene Mims, Vice President for the Church Growth Group, The Sunday School Board.

For almost 20 years, Gene Mims has served as a pastor of Southern Baptist Churches in Texas, Virginia, Alabama, and Tennessee. His calling has been to help churches evangelize the world to Christ, develop believers, and assist churches to grow.

Gene's calling and commitment did not change when he was elected Vice President for the Church Growth Group of the Sunday School Board. In fact, in the providence of God, his calling to serve churches has deepened and broadened with his assignment to serve Southern Baptists.

Under Dr. Mims' direction, the Church Growth Group has become a constant source of fresh and new services to help churches grow and expand their witness to the saving grace of Jesus Christ.

Recently, Dr. Mims told a group of pastors: "The mandate of the Great Commission is our driving force, and our focus is meeting the needs of churches. Though we express this focus in a variety of ministries, our commitment is always and forever to local churches— their pastors, staffs, and individual members."

Dr. Mims is a Master of Divinity and Doctor of Ministry graduate of Southwestern Baptist Theological Seminary. He has served as president of the Southwestern Seminary Alumni for Tennessee and is a frequent writer of Sunday School lessons and numerous other articles for national publications.

Prior to writing *Thine Is the Kingdom,* Mims authored two books— *God's Call to a Corrupt Nation* and *Kingdom Principles for Church Growth.*

Introduction

"To you it has been granted to know the mysteries of the kingdom of heaven" (Matt. 13:11).

This book is written with a simple conviction that the kingdom of God is the fundamental reality operating in our world today. It is the very center of God's present-day activity and is essential to any understanding of our present world and what is to come. Most people do not know or believe this truth. Most believe their lives are ruled and governed by economic, political, social, or technological forces. If they do believe in anything beyond these forces, it is usually some undefined force they may or may not refer to as God. Still others live their lives with a belief in chance or fate. To them life is a gamble. These seek to find the best odds for happiness and fulfillment, and then hope for the best.

Even Christians are sometimes confused about God's activity in the world today. Some even declare that Satan is ruling the earth and universe. This is not the case. He certainly is the ruler of the world-system and leader of those who hate God, but this world belongs to God, and Satan is not able to rule what belongs to God.

This is why we need to discover the kingdom of God for our lives. We need to know the truth about what is happening in our world today as well as what will happen in the future. We will discover in this study that the kingdom of God was founded by the Father to accomplish His purposes, focused in Christ His Son who is its King, and it is facilitated by the Holy Spirit who uses His power to accomplish God's purposes in the world. If we are to live confidently and serve the Lord effectively, we need a biblical worldview and a kingdomview.

The Old Testament prophets predicted the kingdom's coming. John the Baptist announced its imminent appearance, and Jesus Christ declared it with authority and power. The kingdom of God became fully operational in the lives of believers and within the church at Pentecost (see Acts 2) and it has been expanding ever since. The kingdom will be fully realized when Christ returns from heaven to rule on earth with His saints.

The full importance of the kingdom of God has sometimes been lost to believers. To some the kingdom of God is defined as being already fully present within the lives of Christians. Those who have held to this definition usually discount the return of Christ as nonessential or too far away to worry about. Those who follow this belief generally work and focus on the kingdom of God on earth. Ministry for them is focused on the present with little future consequence. This view of the kingdom departs from the teachings of Christ who exhorts us to be ready at any time for His return.

> *"Be dressed in readiness, and keep your lamps alight. And be like men who are waiting for their master when he returns from the wedding feast, so that they may immediately open the door to him when he comes and knocks. Blessed are those slaves whom the master shall find on the alert when he comes. . . . You too be ready; for the Son of Man is coming at an hour that you do not expect"* (Luke 12:35-37, 40).

The return of Christ gives us hope and assurance of God's love and redemptive activity no matter what conditions surround us. To deny the return of Christ is to make the Christian faith a pitiful attempt to give meaning to life which has no meaning. Jesus promised that He will return to earth. We will see Him when He comes. We will enter into His presence as He reigns as King of kings on earth and in heaven.

On the other hand, some have so emphasized the return of Christ that our responsibility to join God in His present-day activity is overlooked or ignored. There is kingdom work to accomplish in our world today which includes joining God on His redemptive mission. God continues to create persons in the world, giving them life and the opportunity to know Him personally. He gives us the opportunity to evangelize them and to offer them His forgiveness of sin and eternal life. He commissions us to go everywhere in our world, not only evangelizing it, but also subduing it for the kingdom's sake. We cannot be relieved of responsibility to make our planet better for those who live on it. God places us in the world to accomplish His purposes. We are to proclaim the gospel to all persons, we are to gather with other believers to worship, to minister, to study, to disciple believers, and to join in fellowship together. But we are also to go back into the world as salt and light to make a difference among those who do not know Christ.

*"You are the salt of the earth; but if the salt has become
tasteless, how will it be made salty again? ... You are the
light of the world. A city set on a hill cannot be hidden. Nor
do men light a lamp, and put it under the peck-measure,
but on the lampstand; and it gives light to all who are in
the house. Let your light shine before men in such a way
that they may see your good works, and glorify your Father
who is in heaven" (Matt. 5:13-16).*

We cannot seek the kingdom of God and the righteousness of God by simply waiting for Christ's return and doing nothing in our world. We must work the works of the Father, seeking to share the gospel with every person, baptize believers, and teach them how to live as followers of Christ. While it is true that we cannot evangelize the world and disciple believers through ministry activities alone, we must not avoid penetrating our world for Christ with ministries which reach people in their immediate needs. All believers have the responsibility to be salt and light wherever God chooses to use them. We are sometimes critical of governmental social agencies, but one reason these institutions are so powerful and influential is because believers have not assumed responsibility in society. A government or social-service agency can never do what Christians are called to do. God expects His people to meet the needs of people and share the hope we have in Christ as we minister.

As believers, we do not need government leaders, social critics, and secular educators to instruct us on the evils of racism, pornography, drug addiction, alcoholism, abuse, and divorce. We have a living relationship with the Creator and Redeemer of the universe who shows us His righteous nature, gives us instruction on moral certainties, and sends us in His power as His messengers to proclaim His gospel and kingdom. His values and ours are the same. We receive from Him understanding about what is wrong in our world and what it takes to make it right. God places governments and leaders of nations in place to rule according to His purposes. We do not object to the role of leaders and institutions in society, but neither can we give them our responsibility to serve the world. We have the Word of God to guide us and the life of Christ within us to do right wherever we are. Whenever the kingdom of God is unleashed through the lives of believers, the institutions of man will find their appropriate place.

It is our hope that as you study the kingdom of God, you might come to understand it and begin to seek it as a life-goal. This seeking will result in Christlikeness, righteousness, joy, and peace in the Holy Spirit. Also, it is our hope that you might join the Father in His redemptive work in the world today. It is your privilege as a child of God to understand what He is doing in the world and to respond to His invitation to join Him in that activity. You have been chosen, called, and set apart for His purposes; your greatest fulfillment in life is to walk with Christ to fulfill those purposes.

Jesus Christ declared, "My Father is working until now, and I Myself am working" (John 5:17). He then called us to the same task that the Father sent Him to accomplish. "We must work the works of Him who sent Me, as long as it is day; night is coming, when no man can work. While I am in the world, I am the light of the world" (John 9:4-5).

When we observe the life and work of Jesus on earth as He inaugurated the kingdom of God, we see how He joined the Father in His works. Jesus never competed with any of the powerful authorities of His day. He never attacked the rulers and governors in the world of the first century. He accepted them as fact and as subject to His Father. He did not attempt to compete with the recognized religious leaders and teachings of the time. He did not try to unseat and overturn the social and economic order. Under the authority given to Him from His Father, He proclaimed the kingdom of God and gave it to persons who would follow Him and bear fruit. He clearly presented the kingdom's principles and called men and women to become kingdom citizens. As they responded and followed Him, He gave them the power to live and work according to the will of God in the world. Anyone who receives the kingdom and gives himself to God by faith in Christ is filled with the Holy Spirit and enabled to share the love of God with others.

You and I have been given the same wonderful relationship with the Father through Christ that believers experienced in the first century. We have been given power and authority, not to bring arguments against those who teach unsound philosophies and theologies, but to preach the gospel of the kingdom of God. Whenever we have the opportunity to meet those who proclaim false doctrine, we can debate and discuss, but our priority is to present Christ, not argue. We have been given authority, not to destroy social structures and political realms, but to change lives and help persons come from the darkness of their sin and separation from God to the light of His love and purposes for their lives. When lives are changed by Christ, then social change will follow soon. We do not have to defend a helpless God and a hopeless Christ. He is King and Lord of all! We have the responsibility to proclaim the kingdom of God which has come in power through Jesus. This kingdom cannot fail or be defeated. Jesus created us to be a prophetic people to live and work for Him to bring His kingdom to fulfillment.

The message of the gospel is filled with power even in the words we use to communicate it. Paul correctly says that the gospel "is the power of God for salvation to everyone who believes" (Rom. 1:16). The message is powerful enough to overcome arguments, sinful minds, immoral lifestyles, and anything else which stands in the way of the advance of the kingdom of God.

In our time, however, we often replace the kingdom of God with other things. We sometimes replace the kingdom of God and its agenda with our own agendas. Church growth issues, mission methods, end-time theories, ministry programs, personal self-improvement, and social and political causes are good things, but they are not priorities over the kingdom of God. In many cases God is pushed aside as we seek to build our churches, our lives, and our own kingdoms. Anything which starts with or centers on man will never focus on the kingdom of God. The lack of resources directing us to intimacy with God and pointing us to His kingdom is proof that we have drifted away from His agenda.

Because we are unaware of the kingdom of God, we encounter the following struggles:

- We have difficulty seeing God at work around us. When He is at work, we often do not understand what or why He does what He does.
- We have no confidence in what Christ has done, is doing, and will do, so we attempt to implement our agendas rather than His.
- We do not pray effectively, go as we are commanded, give support to believers around the world, or endure suffering and hardships as we should.

We must study the kingdom of God from Scripture until a revival occurs within us and we again see God at work and have confidence that Jesus Christ is ruling over all our circumstances. We can make life-adjustments to meet the demands of the kingdom and begin to:

- Set our lives on a course as fully committed disciples as we seek the kingdom first and foremost.
- Pursue an intimate relationship with the Father which results in righteousness and Christlikeness.
- See God at work in our world and adjust every part of our lives to join Him.
- Develop a biblical view of the world.
- Begin to understand evil, suffering, persecution, and injustices in our world, and adjust our lives to deal with them.
- Change the way we look at the local church and its work. We can focus our churches as kingdom agencies to fulfill the Great Commission.

As you work through this study, you will be challenged to adjust your thinking and your life to the realities of the kingdom of God. You will learn new information, and you will be reminded of facts and ideas you have known for many years. It is our wish for you to come into the kind of relationship with the Father which He desires and you need.

Are you willing to look at your life and see if it fits God's kingdom agenda and purposes? Will you examine yourself in the light of God's Word to make any adjustments necessary to develop a kingdomview and a lifestyle to help you meet its demands?

Some persons view the kingdom of God as a resource to use. They name things they want from God on the basis of faith in Christ and His kingdom. Others see the kingdom of God as something to be known and studied. Theological definitions, charts showing the pattern of Christ's return, and endless current event discussions are the focus of their concern. Still others see the kingdom as something to wait for while the world around us decays and sin destroys all except those who believe. In this study we want to move from theories about the kingdom to a dynamic relationship with Christ who is the King and to His reign in our lives which is the kingdom.

The kingdom is not a resource; it is a reality. It is not a doctrine to be discussed but a dynamic to live by. It is not an antidote to a corrupt world but an answer for each of us. It is what moves our universe toward the fulfillment of God's purposes. It is a reality none but those who are in Christ can experience. It is the thing we seek above all else, and it is tied directly to our righteousness in Christ.

As you study the following chapters, you will find your understanding of the kingdom of God will begin to influence your confidence in God's activity. You will begin to see that beyond your circumstances the Lord is working in ways you cannot imagine. Our enemy Satan never wants you to join God in His kingdom work or even to know about the kingdom. Christ defeated Satan at the cross. The resurrection is proof that Jesus Christ is Lord forever. Even though the evil one has power to tempt, provoke, and afflict us, he cannot overcome us. Claim God's Word (all of it) when you feel Satan's pressure. "They overcame him because of the blood of the Lamb and because of the word of their testimony, and they did not love their life even to death" (Rev. 12:11).

Martin Luther penned these famous words:

A mighty fortress is our God, A bulwark never failing;
Our helper He, amid the flood Of mortal ills prevailing:
For still our ancient foe Doth seek to work us woe;
His craft and pow'r are great, And, armed with cruel hate,
On earth is not His equal.

Did we in our own strength confide, Our striving would be losing;
Were not the right Man on our side, The Man of God's own choosing.
Dost ask who that may be? Christ Jesus, it is He;
Lord Sabaoth, His name, From age to age the same,
And He must win the battle.
And tho' this world, with devils filled, Should threaten to undo us,
We will not fear, for God hath willed His truth to triumph thro' us:
The Prince of Darkness grim, We tremble not for him;
His rage we can endure, For lo, his doom is sure,
One little word shall fell him.

That word above all earthly pow'rs, No thanks to them, abideth;
The Spirit and the gifts are ours Thro' Him who with us sideth:

Let goods and kindred go, This moral life also;
The body they may kill: God's truth abideth still,
His Kingdom is forever.

May our confidence and hope in our Father, His Christ, and the Holy Spirit who abides within allow us to discover the fullest meaning of truth—that *His kingdom is forever!*

Throughout this resource you will notice interactive activities for learning. These activities will ask you to respond to statements in the text. Some activities will ask you to think about changing your mind or your behavior to follow God's direction and leading. We have left a wide margin on each page for your note-taking. This resource has been written to help you hear from God as you study His kingdom. It is our earnest hope that you will encounter God as never before, and that you will mark this time in your life as a turning point long after you lay aside the book and move on to another study.

chapter 1

THE KINGDOM OF GOD DEFINED AND PROMISED

chapter 1

THE KINGDOM OF GOD DEFINED AND PROMISED

"Thy kingdom is an everlasting kingdom, and thy dominion endures throughout all generations."

Psalm 145:13

Steve had been an active member and participant in his church, but something had changed. His friends at church noticed that Steve was attending services less frequently. He just did not seem interested. Nobody understood what had caused the change in Steve's involvement in church activities until Bob, a deacon of the church, visited him. When Bob asked Steve if something had gone wrong, or if he was discouraged, Steve sat quietly. After a long and awkward silence, Steve finally responded to Bob's questions. "It's really not anything that anyone has said or done, Bob. The problem is inside me. I was spending a lot of time doing church activities. Then one day I asked myself a question, *Am I hearing anything, learning anything, or doing anything in church that is really making any difference in the way I live my life?* The answer was no! Honestly Bob, I just decided that my life is too full and busy to keep on doing something that doesn't have much effect on daily living."

While most people would not be as direct and honest as Steve, many share his concern. Is there really anything in the way we approach the Christian faith that effects the way we live our lives? Is there some life-changing, motivating center of truth that has the power to make a difference? The answer is yes; the biblical truth about the kingdom of God is that center of truth.

The term *kingdom* is used in the Bible in at least four ways in reference to God. Kingdom sometimes refers to the universal reign of God over all of creation. Because God is sovereign, it is reasonable to understand that He reigns over what He has created. The psalmist says, "The Lord has established His throne in the heavens; and His sovereignty rules over all" (Ps.103:19); "The Lord Most High is to be feared, A great King over all the earth" (Ps. 47:2).

It is important to affirm that God created the heavens and the earth. The impact of secular education in our time has taken the focus away from the personal God who creates the universe for His glory and persons in His own image. The truth of the Bible stands in contrast to evolutionary theories concerning the origins of the universe. These theories lead to the unbiblical conclusion that an impersonal force is responsible for the origin of life. The Bible declares that a person, God Himself, created the universe and all that is in it. God's creating activity gives us understanding of His character and His purposes, and it reveals meaning and significance in our lives. To deny God's creation is essentially to deny His existence. This kind of thinking leads many people to feelings of insignificance.

The Bible also uses the term *kingdom* to describe the nation of Israel. Referring to God's choice of Solomon to rule Israel, David said, "He has chosen my son Solomon to sit on the throne of the kingdom of the Lord over Israel" (1 Chron. 28:5).

God used Israel to reveal His person, His character, His laws, and His purposes. The Israelites were chosen in Abraham, delivered from bondage in Egypt by Moses, led into the promised land by Joshua, and governed by great leaders like Saul, David, and Solomon. The nation was a forerunner or a type of kingdom which God determined to bring to earth in Christ. As a nation or kingdom, Israel was unique and different from other nations. Israel was served by prophets, priests, and kings who worked together to know and do the will of God. They ministered to God's people and helped them to know and obey the Father.

Israel was chosen as a servant to the Lord and to the other nations, not as a ruler over them. Israel was never as powerful or mighty as some other nations. It never had natural resources or favorable geographical features to protect it from invaders and threats. In times of trouble and distress, Israel had only God to defend, bless, and guide it. Israel's well-being was in direct proportion to its relationship to God.

The third and fourth uses of the term *kingdom* in the Bible are closely related, and we will look at them together. These are important definitions which will help us to formulate a comprehensive definition for the term *kingdom of God*.

Kingdom is used in the Bible to describe the present-day activity or rule of God in the world. Jesus began His public ministry by announcing that the kingdom of God had come. His declaration that "the time is fulfilled" meant that Jesus had come to fulfill God's plan to bring His kingdom to earth. It also marked His inauguration as King.

"It is I who made the earth, and created man upon it. I stretched out the heavens with My hands, and I ordained all their host."

Isaiah 45:12

Our understanding of the kingdom of God must be based upon the return of Christ, a dominant theme in the New Testament.

All that God does in the world and in our individual lives is in keeping with His kingdom purpose.

The reign of God invaded time and history in the person of Christ. There is an important difference between persons recognizing that God is the Creator of all things and persons permitting Him to reign in their lives through faith in Christ. God created the world and controls it; at the same time He has redeemed the world, reigns over it, and is actively working out His redemptive purposes.

The fourth use of the term *kingdom* in the Bible refers to the kingdom of God coming at the end of history as we know it. Jesus taught us to pray: "Thy kingdom come. Thy will be done" (Matt. 6:10). This refers to the consummated kingdom of God which will be established at the time of Christ's second coming. This will mark the time when the kingdom of God is fully realized, established, and operational. Sin and evil will be removed from earth; righteousness and peace will be the established order of everyone's life.

Rewind. *List the four ways the word kingdom is used in the Bible.*

1. _____   2. _____

3. _____   4. _____

The four ways that the Bible speaks of the kingdom of God are: God's universal reign over all creation, the nation of Israel, the present day activity of God, and the coming, consummation of the kingdom.

A Definition of the Kingdom

Keeping in mind these four biblical uses of the term *kingdom*, we can offer the following comprehensive definition of the kingdom of God.

> *The kingdom of God is the reign of God through Christ in the lives of persons as evidenced by His activity in, through, and around them. The kingdom was prophesied in the Old Testament, pictured in Israel, proclaimed by John the Baptist, inaugurated by Christ during His public ministry on earth, extended in the lives of believers through the church in the present age, and will be consummated by Christ when He returns to earth to rule with His saints.*

This definition gives us the basis for understanding the kingdom of God from its fullest perspective. We find within it every essential element we need to understand the purposes of God in the world and how His activity today is in keeping with those purposes.

In the following pages we will discover many important aspects of the kingdom of God. We will see that each phrase in the above definition is significant. For now, let's look briefly at each part of the definition. The kingdom of God is:

- *the reign of God through Christ.* You will learn about Christ's significance in both His person and His work and that He is now King of kings and Ruler of all things.
- *evidenced by His activity.* You will learn to recognize the activity of God in, around, and through your life.
- *prophesied in the Old Testament.* We will take a brief survey through the Old Testament and the history of Israel to see how God prepared the world to receive His kingdom through Jesus Christ.
- *proclaimed by John the Baptist.* You will gain an appreciation for John the Baptist who ministered between the end of the Old Testament and the beginning of the New Testament.
- *inaugurated by Christ.* You will learn how Christ's life and ministry on earth marked the beginning of God's reign in the world.
- *extended in the lives of believers.* You will see how your relationship with Christ is the actual extension of the kingdom of God to all the world today.
- *consummated by Christ when He returns.* You will be able to put the return of Christ into a proper perspective as you discover its importance for daily life, ministry, and missions.

This definition will allow us to focus on four important dimensions of the kingdom of God.

In Scripture we see God's activity in both creation and redemption.

Stop and Think! *Every word in the definition of the kingdom is packed with meaning. Read the definition again. Circle the words you consider to be the most important. Underline phrases which include new ideas you have not previously understood as part of a definition for the kingdom of God. Write questions you have about the author's definition.*

1. _____

2. _____

Understanding the fact of sin and God's activity in Christ to redeem lost humanity sets the stage for our understanding of the kingdom of God.

From the Old Testament we will discover the relationship between the kingdom of God and the fall of Adam and Eve. When sin entered the picture, God immediately began to act to bring humankind back into a personal relationship with Himself. From the ministry of Christ we will discover how God's activity has come directly through Jesus to our present world. We will see how His death and resurrection, along with the coming of the Holy Spirit, have brought God's reign to our lives. We also will examine the role of the church in reference to the kingdom of God. We will see that a local church must understand the kingdom of God if it is to function as God intends and join Him on mission in the world. Finally, we will examine Christ's return and its significance. These four aspects of the kingdom of God lay the groundwork for God's coming reign. They also demonstrate that the kingdom is presently in operation with the church as its primary agent and assure us that the kingdom will be consummated at the end of time.

The Kingdom of God in the Old Testament

We will begin by examining the kingdom of God in the Old Testament as the groundwork for the coming of Christ.

FROM ADAM TO ABRAHAM

For us to understand the kingdom of God we must go back to the beginning of recorded history to identify the need for a kingdom. The Bible teaches the following:

- God's existence
- God's character as holy and perfect
- God's activity as purposeful in creation, redemption, and rule
- Man as God's highest and most important earthly creature
- Man as having meaning and purpose in relationship to God
- Man's sin and need of salvation
- Man's responsibility and inability to save himself
- God's single provision for salvation in Christ alone
- Salvation as a sovereign, gracious act of God

Let's look back at Adam and Eve in the garden of Eden and see how these facts begin to play out in God's activity. Biblical history is simple and swift. God created man and woman to live in relationship and enjoy fellowship with Him and with each other. He placed them in a perfect environment to rule over and enjoy. They were free to do as they pleased with only one exception. They were forbidden to eat from one particular tree strategically located in the middle of the garden of Eden. Not long after creation, however, both Adam and Eve sinned against God by eating fruit from the tree God had forbidden. The first couple was tempted by Satan presenting himself as a serpent. When Eve ate the forbidden fruit and shared it with Adam, everything on earth changed for them and for us.

When Adam and Eve sinned, they experienced a number of occurrences and feelings which changed their lives from what they knew in the garden. They experienced spiritual loss because they lost free access and relationship with God. Adam and Eve were soul mates with God and with each other. The Lord literally blew life into Adam's flesh and that same life was given to Eve.

Notice how Genesis describes Adam's creation by God: "Then the Lord God formed man of dust from the ground, and breathed into his nostrils the breath of life; and man became a living being" (Gen. 2:7).

The word translated *being* is literally *soul*. After sinning, Adam and Eve "hid themselves from the presence of the Lord God among the trees of the garden" (Gen. 3:8). Their free access to God was forfeited by their disobedience. Their fellowship was broken, His image within them destroyed, and God's purposes for their lives ruined. Sin made them strangers to God and no longer soul mates. Scripture is explicit that each person, like the first man and woman, has a body, but is a soul.

We are sinners by nature and by choice, so we are alienated from God, even as Adam and Eve were.

Adam and Eve also lost their innocence. God never intended that Adam and Eve should gain knowledge of evil through experience. He gave them freedom to obey Him and His commandments or to disobey Him. Through disobedience they lost good by knowing evil and gained an evil conscience. They became self-conscious, ashamed, and fearful.

Finally, they lost their place. God "sent him [and his wife] out from the garden of Eden, to cultivate the ground from which he was taken. So He drove the man out" (Gen. 3:23-24). Away from the tree of life, they were subject to life at risk as death slowly began creeping toward them. In a word, the first man and woman were lost. They lost everything they had going for them—their lives, their innocence, and their place. Because Adam and Eve lost these things, each of us came into the world with a sinful nature. Scripture certainly is correct when it declares, "There is no man who does not sin" (2 Chron. 6:36).

Despite their sin and failure, God was not finished with Adam and

Eve. He immediately set into motion a plan to reverse what had occurred—a plan of salvation which simultaneously would allow Him to punish sin and forgive the sinner. This plan would be accomplished in Jesus Christ. Notice God's words to Satan in the garden after he had deceived the first man and woman.

> *And the Lord God said to the serpent,*
> *"Because you have done this,*
> *Cursed are you more than all cattle,*
> *And more than every beast of the field;*
> *On your belly shall you go,*
> *And dust shall you eat*
> *All the days of your life;*
> *And I will put enmity*
> *Between you and the woman*
> *And between your seed and her seed;*
> *He shall bruise you on the head,*
> *And you shall bruise him on the heel" (Gen. 3:14-15).*

God's rule, disrupted by Satan's lies and man's sin, would one day be restored in man's relationship to God. Evil and the evil one would be destroyed. The sinner would have opportunity to be saved!

However, the early chapters of human history did not look very promising. After Adam and Eve sinned, Abel was murdered by his brother Cain. Events in the lives of persons living after Cain led to worsening conditions throughout the earth. Finally, God had endured enough and Scripture records the tragic conclusion.

Together the sins of disobedience, anger, and pride had put the human race in a state of danger which seemed insurmountable.

> *Then the Lord saw that the wickedness of man was great on*
> *the earth, and that every intent of the thoughts of his heart*
> *was only evil continually.*
> *And the Lord was sorry that He had made man on the*
> *earth, and He was grieved in His heart.*
> *And the Lord said, "I will blot out man whom I have*
> *created from the face of the land,... But Noah found favor*
> *in the eyes of the Lord (Gen. 6:5-8).*

The destruction of the world by flood meant that humankind could begin again and enter into a new relationship with God. But it was not to be. In sinful pride people built a tower to mark the importance of humankind on earth. God separated persons from one another by confusing their languages and scattering them across the face of the earth. From Adam to the Tower of Babel, the condition of the people on earth seemed hopeless.

God's grace, however, is not dependent on human goodness nor destroyed by human sinfulness. He made a promise to Adam and Eve, and His Word can never be broken or changed. Genesis 12 records the dramatic story of the call of Abram, better known to us as Abraham. God promised descendants and a land to Abraham and Sarah. Despite their personal difficulties and a prolonged wait, God blessed them with a son, Issac. Issac fathered Jacob who was father to Joseph. Issac and Jacob both received from God the same promise Abraham had received, namely that He would bless them, their descendants, and make a great people of them. Joseph's brothers shamefully sold him into slavery in Egypt, where ultimately famine brought the family together again. Although their physical needs were met and the family was reunited, their sin against Joseph meant four hundred years of slavery for God's people. From Adam's sin to Israel's slavery, God's purposes seemed to face defeat. His people struggled without leadership, hope, or understanding. Their needs appeared to be much greater than resources and solutions.

The Bible makes it clear that the work of God is not dependent on human goodness, nor can it be destroyed by human sinfulness.

Stop and Think! *The needs of our world today also seem much greater than resources and solutions. List several pressing problems in your community which seem impossible to solve.*

_____

_____

GOD'S KINGDOM ACTIVITY THROUGH THE MINISTRY OF MOSES

God called Moses to lead the people of God in their exodus from Egypt. Moses was at first reluctant, but eventually he followed God, and the Israelites left Egypt in a dramatic and miraculous fashion. Three months into their journey from Egypt to Canaan, Moses met with God on Mount Sinai. This encounter is one of the most significant in all of Scripture because we see for the first time how God's promises to Adam and Eve, Abraham, Issac, Jacob, and Moses were to be fulfilled. We also see the nature of God's activity as He acted to redeem His creation.

"The Lord said: 'I have surely seen the affliction of My people who are in Egypt, and have given heed to their cry because of their taskmasters, for I am aware of their sufferings. So I have come down to deliver them from the power of the Egyptians, and to bring them up from that land to a good and spacious land, to a land flowing with milk and honey.... Therefore, come now, and I will send you to Pharaoh, so that you may bring My people, the sons of Israel, out of Egypt.'"

Exodus 3:7-8,10

Exodus 19–24 have often been called the most important chapters in the entire Old Testament because they demonstrate the nature of God in relationship to His people as well as His purposes. Exodus 19:1-6 is a pivotal passage in understanding God's redemptive purposes as He acts to redeem His people from sin and bring them into His kingdom. God instructed Moses to tell the Israelites the following:

"You yourselves have seen what I did to the Egyptians, and how I bore you on eagles' wings, and brought you to Myself. Now then, if you will indeed obey My voice and keep My covenant, then you shall be My own possession among all the peoples, for all the earth is Mine; And you shall be to Me a kingdom of priests and a holy nation" (Ex.19:4-6).

There are three promises in this text which are significant because they reappear in the New Testament and are an integral part of the heritage of anyone who follows Christ. First, God promises that His children will be His own possession. God chooses to treasure and value His people as His personal and most delightful possession. Second, God promises that His people will be a kingdom of priests to Him. The priesthood of believers means that every believer has immediate and direct access to God, as well as the responsibility to minister to others. Third, God promises to make His people a holy nation which means that believers are set apart from others to reflect the nature and purposes of God.

At this point, we will focus on the second promise which reveals God's intention to make of His people a kingdom. For the first time in Scripture and the last time in the Old Testament, the term *kingdom* is used to mean the reign of God in the lives of His people enabling them to serve God completely and to enjoy complete and free access to Him. Priests stand between men and God and offer something to each for the sake of the other. To man, the Israelites were to offer the knowledge of the light of God. To God, they were to offer praise, sacrifice, and obedience.

The Lord has not made us priests unto Him because of anything we can do for Him. We are priests to Him because He wants us to offer ourselves to Him in relationship and service for His purposes. We, like Israel, have no greatness in ourselves except from God and His grace to us.

Rewind. *What important truth is first mentioned in Exodus 19:1-6?*

_____

_____

The truth that God's people are a kingdom of priests, first mentioned in this Old Testament passage, is extremely important in our understanding of the way God works through His people. These verses reveal three indicators of God's activity which are found throughout the Bible. Simply stated they are: God creates, God redeems, and God enters into a personal relationship with persons.

First, God reminded Moses that all the earth is His (v. 5). He created it for His pleasure and His purposes. We cannot separate God the Creator from God the Redeemer. He is God and Creator, so all things and all persons are His. He made them according to His own purposes and He claims them for Himself. Others may seek to conquer the world, its territories, and its people, but God alone possesses them.

The second indication of the nature of God's activity is His redemptive work. God is Creator of all persons, but He is only Father and Lord to those who are redeemed. God delivered His people from the hands of the Egyptians. He redeemed them from slavery and their hopeless condition to give them new life and a land of their own. He did not want them to be in bondage and outside His rule. Pharaoh's rule over the people of God was improper and had to end.

The third indication of God's activity is His desire to be in a personal relationship with His people. He told Moses to tell the children of Israel that God "bore you on eagles' wings, and brought you to Myself" (v.4). God did not deliver His people only because they were slaves or to give them a land of their own. He did not choose them because they were pure or worthy of His attention. He chose them out of His desire to have a relationship with them collectively and individually.

The surprising revelation in Scripture is not that God is working to redeem humankind from sin and death. We would expect Him to do that as a loving Father and Creator. The surprise is that God purposes to invite men and women to join Him in His work. God chose to do His work through Israel. The only condition for the people was their obedience to Him. It was as simple for them as it is for us. God works

The people of God who live under His rule become priests to Him.

"The earth is the Lord's, and all it contains, The world, and those who dwell in it."

Psalm 24:1

to redeem the world through persons who choose to obey Him. If Israel would obey Him, they would be blessed above all nations. But their privilege would be even greater than their blessings. They would be His priests, and God would work to accomplish His purposes through them.

Rewind. *Complete the following sentence. It is not surprising that a loving God would redeem people, but that He would _____ men and women ___ _____ Him in _____ _____ is the surprise!*

God is a loving King who throughout history creates persons to have a relationship with them despite their sin and rebellion.

The really wonderful and surprising truth is that God would not only love people enough to save them from their sin, but that He would invite those who are saved to join Him in His work.

ISRAEL'S RISE AND FALL

We need to take a brief look at the fortunes of Israel as a nation. They show us how the purposes of God prevail despite the sinfulness and weakness of God's people. God's covenant with Israel was simple. If the people obeyed Him and kept His commandments, He would bless them and care for all their needs. He would protect them and provide for them and use them to complete His purposes in the world. Israel possessed a deep sense of calling and destiny from its covenant with God, but eventually the people took it for granted. They did not uphold their commitment to God, but expected that He would always uphold His to them.

Israel's history as the people of God is neither long nor illustrious. From the time of their wandering in the wilderness to the last days of both Judah and Israel, the people rebelled against God and His rule over their lives. In fact, Israel only lasted as a nation through her first three kings. Saul, David, and Solomon ruled a united nation, but after Solomon died the people were divided, conquered, and eventually destroyed. Despite the heroic efforts of some good kings, some godly priests, and some powerful prophets, the nation declined and disintegrated.

As we look at the events in Scripture from Moses to Malachi, we begin to develop a biblical perspective which views things in the long-term sense. In the short term, at times, it appears as if the work of God is failing, but in the long term, we realize it cannot. The kingdom of God is not dependent upon the righteousness and faithfulness of God's people. We cannot destroy God's work in our world simply because we are not the people we should be. Likewise, conditions which threaten us do not threaten God.

Stop and Think! *Describe a time in your past when it seemed as if the work of God was failing, but later you realized God was at work throughout the difficulty.*

_____

_____

The enemies of God, ruled and ruined by Satan, will not and cannot overcome the purposes of God. Circumstances do not dictate to God; instead, He controls the circumstances.

During the years of Israel's greatness, the Father began to reveal a coming Messiah or Anointed One Who would be a Prophet, Priest, and King for all the world. Moses saw it, the prophets saw it, and even some of the people recognized His coming. The Old Testament pictures Jehovah God as the King of His people. Leaders such as Gideon and Samuel recognized that only God can be King over His people.

> *Then the men of Israel said to Gideon, "Rule over us, … for you have delivered us from the hand of Midian." But Gideon said to them, "I will not rule over you, nor shall my son rule over you; the Lord shall rule over you" (Judg. 8:22-23).*
>
> *Then all the elders of Israel gathered together and came to Samuel at Ramah; and they said to him, … "Now appoint a king for us to judge us like all the nations." But the thing was displeasing in the sight of Samuel (1 Sam. 8:4-6).*

Despite their warnings, the people persisted and God allowed them to have a ruler. Saul, then David, followed by Solomon were the first kings of Israel. Saul began to consolidate the tribes into a unified group; David reigned over the first legitimate monarchy; and Solomon guided Israel throughout its most glorious times. Following Solomon's death, however, the nation divided into two nations. Some estimate that David began ruling in 1000 B.C. and Israel fell in 731 B.C. with Judah following in 586 B.C. This is not a long and glorious history for a people chosen by God as a prized possession, a kingdom of priests, and a people set apart for His purposes.

While Israel decayed and Judah diminished over the centuries, God raised up and anointed prophets to call the people to obedience.

The sins of Adam and Eve, the wickedness of Noah's day, and the pride of the Tower of Babel continued to plague God's people until they were destroyed. But their destruction did not come without God's pleading for them to return to Him. Notice some of the words of pleading and warning from the prophets.

> *"Has the Lord as much delight in burnt offerings and*
> *sacrifices*
> *As in obeying the voice of the Lord?" (1 Sam. 15:22).*

> *"Come now, and let us reason together,"*
> *Says the Lord,*
> *"Though your sins are as scarlet,*
> *They will be as white as snow;*
> *Though they are red like crimson,*
> *They will be like wool.*
> *"If you consent and obey,*
> *You will eat the best of the land;*
> *"But if you refuse and rebel,*
> *You will be devoured by the sword" (Isa. 1:18-20).*

> *"But this is what I commanded them, saying, 'Obey My*
> *voice, and I will be your God, and you will be My people;*
> *and you will walk in all the way which I command you,*
> *that it may be well with you' " (Jer. 7:23).*

Isaiah, like the other prophets, called the people to return to the Lord.

> *"Seek the Lord while He may be found;*
> *Call upon Him while He is near.*
> *Let the wicked forsake his way*
> *And the unrighteous man his thoughts;*
> *and let him return to the Lord,*
> *And he will have compassion on him;*
> *And to our God,*
> *For He will abundantly pardon" (Isa. 55:6-7).*

Over and over again the prophets called Israel to repentance and away from idols, immorality, and sinfulness.

God pled for His people to remember the covenant and how He had chosen them and made them a nation to fulfill His purposes and to share His life. With the covenant came obligations which Israel did not keep. The covenant promises God made were alive and dynamic, but they were not automatic. Israel took her election, calling, and destiny by Jehovah for granted. In the end, her sin and rebellion was too much. The swiftness of the fall of God's people is reminiscent of Proverbs 29:1.

> *"A man who hardens his neck after much reproof*
> *Will suddenly be broken beyond remedy."*

God did not fail in His purposes, although Israel failed to obtain all the Lord had purposed. Israel fell short while God moved forward to change history.

Even before the fall of Israel and Judah and the captivity of the people of God, the prophets, inspired by the Holy Spirit, began to sense and to see a new covenant in God's mind and heart. This covenant did not center upon the ability of God's people to honor it. Rather, God Himself would make it possible for them to do His will and obey His Word. Parallel to this was the truth that Israel as a nation could never be equated with the kingdom of God.

Rewind. *Mark the following statements T (true) or F (false).*

___ *Even in the Old Testament, the prophets wrote of a coming kingdom that would be broader than Israel.*

___ *Israel failed to keep its obligations under the covenant God established.*

___ *The failure of Israel to honor the covenant was an indication that God's plan had failed.*

The first two statements above are true. The third is false. Israel's failure to fulfill its mission did not mean that God's plan had failed.

ISRAEL'S FAILURE AND GOD'S PLAN

Jeremiah offers the best contrast between Israel's failure and God's future.

> *"Thus says the Lord,*
> *'Cursed is the man who trusts in mankind*
> *And makes flesh his strength,*
> *And whose heart turns away from the Lord' " (Jer.17:5).*

> *"Behold, days are coming," declares the Lord, "when I will make a new covenant with the house of Israel and with the house of Judah, not like the covenant which I made with their fathers in the day I took them by the hand to bring*

While Israel struggled in its sin, God continued His plan to bring about His reign on earth in the lives of His people.

29

*them out of the land of Egypt, My covenant which they
broke. ... But this is the covenant which I will make with
the house of Israel after those days," declares the Lord, "I
will put My law within them, and on their heart I will write
it; and I will be their God, and they shall be My people" (Jer.
31:31-33).*

God was taking something old and making something new which
would be for all peoples and for all times. Israel was proof that no
person or people could keep the law and covenant of God in their
own strength. This is impossible because we are sinners. If God is to
have a kingdom of persons totally devoted to Him, He must do
something to make it possible. No longer could His people be
expected to live with and for Him in their own strength. He must
come to them and dwell among them. He must live life fully with
them. In addition, sin continued to control the lives of God's people.

How could God punish the sin and remove its guilt? Isaiah saw it
clearly when He prophesied:

*"All of us like sheep have gone astray,
Each of us has turned to his own way;
But the Lord has caused the iniquity of us all
To fall on Him.
My Servant, will justify the many,
As He will bear their iniquities" (Isa. 53:6,11).
"For this is like the days of Noah to Me;
When I swore that the waters of Noah
Should not flood the earth again,
So I have sworn that I will not be angry with you,
Nor will I rebuke you.
"For the mountains may be removed and the hills may
shake,
But My lovingkindness will not be removed from you,
And My covenant of peace will not be shaken,"
Says the Lord who has compassion on you" (Isa. 54:9-10).*

*The kingdom was coming and
would be wider and broader than
Israel could ever be. It would not
exclude Israel or anyone else, but it
would be different.*

Who is this servant who brings the covenant of peace? Jesus Christ,
the Messiah.

While the nation of Israel proved that on its own it could not fulfill
its relationship with God, God was moving to complete His already

established plan. It was a plan to bring salvation to every person in the world. It was a plan whereby men and women could enter into an intimate personal relationship with Him forever.

The first step to seeing God at work is to focus on God and not on yourself or your circumstances. The second step is to study the Scriptures to learn about God and His ways. In the Old Testament we see God at work despite the failure of His people to hear, understand, and obey Him. Outwardly, things regressed as Israel sinned more, but behind the veil of the unseen, God worked to bring His kingdom to earth.

We may look at the condition of our nation and our world today and wonder if God is truly at work. You might look at your own life and ask, *Where are you, Lord?* But God's activity is not seen nor measured by looking first at ourselves or our circumstances. We must remember that He alone is sovereign and works His purposes to completion in His own way and in His own time.

Even when His people do not faithfully abide in His presence and obey Him, He works in other ways and with other people to accomplish His purposes.

After 1947, the communists were in firm control of China. The communist government expelled all missionaries from the country. The faithful missionaries who were forced to leave feared that the work they left behind would be destroyed by the power of communism throughout the land. Forty years later when China was once again opened to foreign visitors, those who returned found a vibrant body of believers that some estimated to be over eighty million strong. God's work was not stopped by communism, and it cannot be stopped by any force on earth.

Stop and Think! *What current circumstances are obscuring your view of God's work in your life? List them in the margin.*

God does not have an alternate plan to bring His purposes into reality. He began long ago to bring salvation to persons; it is His mission and the focus of His activity. Nothing can stop Him from fulfilling His desire to be in a personal relationship with every person who will accept His offer of eternal and abundant life. Read the experiences of Israel and develop a confidence that God will accomplish His purposes instead of looking at circumstances for assurances that He is there and caring for us. The story of Israel is a word portrait detailing the condition of our lives apart from God's help and presence. We have the assurance of His Word each day that He will do as He has said.

From the Old Testament we learn of God's faithfulness, perseverance, and power to accomplish what He intends.

The Old Testament closed in darkness and shame for the people of God. The nation of Israel had fallen; God's people were under the rule of others. The leaders of Israel, the priests, prophets, and kings were not able to lead Israel away from sin or back to greatness. The people of God cried out for a priest to represent them before God, a king to lead them away from their destruction, or a prophet to speak God's Word to them. For 400 years the nation had no one to fulfill these roles. Despite this, the prophet Daniel looked far into the future and saw something while in the presence of Belshazzar, king of Babylon.

> *"I kept looking in the night visions,*
> *And behold, with the clouds of heaven*
> *One like a Son of Man was coming,*
> *And He came up to the Ancient of Days*
> *And was presented before Him.*
> *"And to Him was given dominion,*
> *Glory and a kingdom,*
> *That all the peoples, nations, and men of every language*
> *Might serve Him.*
> *His dominion is an everlasting dominion*
> *Which will not pass away;*
> *And His kingdom is one*
> *Which will not be destroyed" (Dan. 7:13-14).*

Daniel saw the Father establish a kingdom, reign, and dominion which would be for everyone and last forever. Within the kingdom the people of the Son of man gathered to serve Him forever. It was a kingdom which could never be destroyed.

The prophetic clock began to tick away the seconds, minutes, hours, and years until the Son of man appeared. Neither the sins of Israel nor God's seeming silence would prevent the kingdom of God from suddenly appearing on earth.

Chapter 2

THE KINGDOM COME

chapter 2

THE KINGDOM COME

The Old Testament concludes with Israel ruled by the Persians and led by Darius II. The New Testament opens with Judea under Roman rule and emperor Caesar Augustus. The four hundred years between the two testaments was a time of world change, conquest of nations, and social development. Lost to biblical history during those years was the activity of God who was working to bring the kingdom to earth. In this chapter we will see that in spite of years of silence, God worked to fulfill His purposes in history. The kingdom of God exploded on earth and ignited the manifestation of God's work among humanity. Also we will look at the person of Christ, together with His ministry and His teachings about the kingdom of God, to see how God brought salvation to us in Christ.

It all began with a man named John …

The Forerunner Comes

The prophet Malachi gave the people of God His final admonition, and with it the promise of one who would come before the Messiah.

> *"Remember the law of Moses My servant, even the statutes and ordinances which I commanded him in Horeb for all Israel.*
>
> *Behold, I am going to send you Elijah the prophet before the coming of the great and terrible day of the Lord.*
>
> *And he will restore the hearts of the fathers to their children, and the hearts of the children to their fathers, lest I come and smite the land with a curse"* (Mal. 4:4-6).

Now in those days John the Baptist came, preaching in the wilderness of Judea, saying, "Repent, for the kingdom of heaven is at hand."

Matthew 3:1-2

Malachi 3:1 tells of a messenger who will prepare the way for the Messiah. This messenger, identified as Elijah in 4:5, is obviously John the Baptist. John was born to Zacharias and Elizabeth and was described by the angel Gabriel in this manner.

> *"You will give him the name John. And you will have joy and gladness, and many will rejoice at his birth. For he will*

*be great in the sight of the Lord, and he will drink no wine
or liquor; and he will be filled with the Holy Spirit, while yet
in his mother's womb. And he will turn back many of the
sons of Israel to the Lord their God. And it is he who will go
as a forerunner before Him in the spirit and power of
Elijah, to turn the hearts of the fathers back to the children,
and the disobedient to the attitude of the righteous; so as to
make ready a people prepared for the Lord" (Luke 1:13-17).*

Notice the mission of John the Baptist: "to turn the hearts of the
fathers back to the children, and the disobedient to the attitude of the
righteous." This would prepare the people to receive the coming Lord
and bring peace between fathers and their children when repentance
was complete. Even the disobedient would have a change of heart
toward obeying God and following Him. It is little wonder that
Zacharias had trouble understanding. He and Elizabeth were too old
to have children and perhaps had a difficult time comprehending
such a powerful message.

John preached a message of repentance and forgiveness of sins.
He baptized persons who repented. He challenged the religious rulers
of his day to repent and to show their repentance by living changed
lives. To those who heard him, there was no doubt that he was the
one Isaiah spoke of who came "crying" in the wilderness, calling for
the people of God to prepare for the coming of the Messiah. The
most amazing message John preached was, "Repent, for the kingdom
of heaven is at hand" (Matt. 3:2). This message is short but powerful
in its importance. *Repent* is a word that means *to change one's mind
about something.* Some believe that repentance means only to
experience a feeling of sorrow regarding some wrong or sinful act.
Repentance naturally carries the idea of remorse for sin, but John
called upon persons to change their hearts, minds, and ways. The
doorway to the kingdom is repentance and belief that God's Word is
true and must be obeyed.

The object of repentance is important also. You can change your
mind about anything, and your opinion can still be wrong. John
called for persons to examine their lives and then to change their
minds about the coming kingdom of God. He linked the imminent
coming of the Messiah to his hearer's repentance. Like John's
appearance, his message was a shock to the people who came to the
wilderness to hear him.

*"A voice is calling,
'Clear the way for the
Lord in the wilderness;
Make smooth in the desert
a highway for our God.
'Let every valley be
lifted up,
And every mountain and
hill be made low;
And let the rough ground
become a plain,
And the rugged terrain a
broad valley;
Then the glory of the Lord
will be revealed,
And all flesh will see it
together;
For the mouth of the Lord
has spoken.' "*

Isaiah 40:3-5

Rewind. *Mark the following statements T (true) or F (false).*
___ *Repent means to change your mind about something.*

___ *Repentance includes remorse for sin.*

___ *Repentance includes a change in behavior.*

John's message of repentance was a call for his hearers to change their minds about their sin, but it was more. When a person repents he experiences remorse for his sin, but most importantly, this change of mind and experience of remorse leads to a change in behavior.

The time was right for God to bring His Son to earth, but there must have been many who wondered if John's ministry was truly of God. No one could be blamed for not observing God at work while reading the Old Testament prophecies and then comparing them to the early years of the first century. But remember, God works in ways we do not see and often do not understand. Who ever would have thought He would commission a figure like John the Baptist to announce the coming of the Messiah? Who could have anticipated John's message of repentance and the forgiveness of sins? John was the forerunner of the Messiah; yet his ministry was so powerful and influential that some thought he *was* the Messiah. Each Gospel writer took time to point out that John's role was that of forerunner to Christ, announcing and preparing the way of the One who would come soon.

John's ministry marked the fulfillment of the Old Testament hope and prophecy; his death marked the beginning of the Messiah's earthly ministry. What God purposed in the Old Testament was becoming reality in the world. The kingdom, prefigured in David's reign, would become reality in Jesus' ministry. Israel's hope rested on the coming King. The world was prepared by the providence of the Father to receive the Son. The Son of man, Jesus Christ, who came to take away the sins of the world, would be the focus of the kingdom. Zacharias understood it first when at John's birth he declared:

> *"Blessed be the Lord God of Israel,*
> *For He has visited us and accomplished redemption for His people...*
> *To give to His people the knowledge of salvation*
> *By the forgiveness of their sins*

Jesus called John the Baptist the greatest human being to live on earth before He inaugurated the kingdom of heaven. He identified him as the Elijah who had been promised (Matt. 11:11,13-14).

Because of the tender mercy of our God
With which the Sunrise from on high shall visit us" (Luke
1:68, 77-78).

Redemption, salvation, peace, and hope follow John's message and ministry.

How would you have responded to the message of John the Baptist? It is an important question because his life and ministry point to the different ways God works in our world. There was nothing appealing about John the Baptist. His clothing was odd, his ways eccentric, his message too hard for most to bear, and his methods too primitive. Yet, his impact was enormous. He was set apart by God for His purposes and anointed by God in the power of the Holy Spirit to become the greatest of men.

Stop and Think! *Imagine you were alive and experienced the ministry of John the Baptist. List some words which describe how you might have responded to him.*

_____

_____

_____

_____

_____

God is not bound to use who we are or what we determine as necessary to achieve His purposes. He is not dependent upon our funding, supporting, or planning to make His redemptive impact on the world. John had no resources and no certain future, but He was God's chosen person to bring the kingdom message.

You may be sure that as God works around you daily, He does so out of His own character and in ways that He deems best. You also may be sure that His ways and methods are not easy to see and understand because they are different from what we might expect.

God made you to be a unique person in order to have fellowship with you and to use you to fulfill His purposes.

His Word says He is different (Isa. 55:8), and we must not expect to be able to determine what He will do and how He will do it. John was a witness, a light, a preacher, and a leader chosen to bring persons to Christ. God picked Him to do a great work, and in wilderness obscurity, he accomplished his task.

His life was completely set apart for whatever God wanted to say and do through him. His greatness should be ours. Are we willing to make ourselves available to do anything or go anywhere God might choose? He is building a kingdom and calls us to change our thinking about the way we live and what we do for Him. As you study this chapter, ask God to open your heart to His message. He is drawing you into a deeper relationship with Him as you seek His kingdom.

Stop and Think! *Reading a challenge to respond personally to God's call to His kingdom and responding personally are not the same! Take time now to meditate on the question in the text, "Are you willing to make yourself available to do anything or go anywhere God might choose?" Compose a prayer reflecting your answer in the space below.*

_____

_____

_____

_____

_____

"And after John had been taken into custody, Jesus came into Galilee, preaching the gospel of God, and saying, 'The time is fulfilled, and the kingdom of God is at hand; repent and believe in the gospel.' "

Mark 1:14-15

Inauguration of the King

Jesus preached a similar message as John the Baptist with some important additions. He added the "gospel of God" (Mark 1:14) to help His hearers understand that His message was from God and it was the good news that they had been promised centuries before. His message was God's good news to them through Him. Jesus also added that the message was being shared because "the time is fulfilled." In fact, the wording points to the precise point where God broke into history and revealed Himself in His Son and His message.

Jesus also called for faith in the message of God's good news and related repentance and faith just as John the Baptist had done.

The message was clear—but what about this kingdom that John and Jesus preached? How did it affect the lives of their hearers and how does it affect us? Most of us are not familiar with the nature and function of a kingdom. United States citizens enjoy a democracy governed by the will of the people. We elect our leaders and they remain in office only as they please the majority of those they serve. We have a president, not a king, to lead our nation; we have legislators, not prophets, to make and give us laws; and we have judges, not priests, to assure fair treatment. In fact, we overthrew the rule of an English king to eventually become a democratic nation.

The subjects of the kingdom of God are those who enter into a relationship with the Father through faith in the Son.

For many centuries people were ruled by kings and queens. Monarchies existed in many nations until the 18th-century revolutions when democratic governments were formed throughout Europe. It is helpful to review the elements of a kingdom as we begin to understand the significance of the kingdom of God for our lives.

Obviously, a kingdom requires a king, a ruler, or a sovereign who is able and willing to rule. A king's rule is required because people need leadership, protection, and provision. A king also is responsible for the overall welfare of his people to assure they live in the best possible environment. A king must have subjects or people to rule. Without people there is no need for a king. A kingdom also must have a domain, a place, or a sphere over which to rule. Most of the time this domain is geographical, but some kings actually rule in exile. A kingdom must have a purpose—a compelling reason which requires a king. And a king must have power and be able to exercise it to govern and protect his people from harm. Without power, rule is impossible.

Rewind. *In the preceding paragraph, find and list below as many key words as you can find which identify elements of a kingdom.*

_____ _____

_____ _____

_____ _____

You probably listed words such as: sovereign, ruler, leadership, protection, provision, subjects, domain, purpose, and power. These

In the resurrection of Christ, all enemies of God and man were defeated finally and decisively.

same elements are present in the kingdom of God. When Jesus began His ministry and announced that the kingdom of God had come to earth, all the elements of a kingdom were present. God was—and is King. We remember from our Old Testament study that God was king of Israel—not Saul, David, or Solomon. Since God has always been King, Jesus announced the kingdom's *appearance* on earth, not its beginning. Because Jesus is God who became man, it is natural for Him to have the title King. Pilate asked if He were a king and then asked the crowd, "Shall I crucify your King?" (John 19:15). In the Book of Revelation Paul addressed seven churches in the name of "Jesus Christ, the faithful witness, the first-born of the dead, and the ruler of the kings of the earth" (Rev. 1:5). Speaking of Jesus, the angel said to Mary, "His kingdom will have no end" (Luke 1:33).

Both Jesus and John the Baptist preached repentance and faith for the forgiveness of sins. The kingdom of God focuses on Jesus Christ as the One who brings forgiveness of sin and redemption when we repent, place our trust in Him, and invite Him into our lives.

The kingdom of God is not limited to earthly geography nor by earthly boundaries. In a sense the kingdom of God is invisible because God reigns within the hearts and lives of believers. The kingdom is real, however, not imaginary. Jesus said: "The kingdom of God is not coming with signs to be observed; nor will they say, 'Look, here it is!' or, 'There it is!' For behold, the kingdom of God is in your midst" (Luke 17:20-21). The kingdom lives within us until the time that Jesus will consumate it at His second coming.

The purpose of the kingdom of God is the redemption of the world. Since the fall of Adam and Eve into sin, God has worked to bring His salvation to the world. He did this through Jesus' death on the cross and His ressurection. Everything about the kingdom of God relates to Jesus' relationship with people who come to know Him through Christ. The kingdom of God is the rule of God in the hearts and lives of people who accept and follow Him on earth, but live with Him forever.

The power of the kingdom of God was demonstrated continually in Jesus' life and ministry. Later we will look at this truth in more detail, but we can observe His power to heal, exorcise demons, teach and preach with authority, and to work miracles. God's greatest display of power, however, was in the resurrection of Christ.

Rewind. *Complete the following sentences to summarize the key elements of the kingdom of God.*

The king of the kingdom of God is _____

The subjects of the kingdom of God are _____

The domain of the kingdom of God is _____

The purpose of the kingdom of God is _____

The Bible teaches that the kingdom of God is the rule of God. The subjects of this kingdom are the people of God. The domain of God's kingdom is not a specific geographical area. His kingdom is wherever His rule is acknowledged. God has a very specific purpose for His kingdom. That purpose is to redeem all who will come to Him.

Jesus Christ the Person

Jesus began His public ministry by announcing the kingdom of God had come to earth. This announcement marked His inauguration—the beginning of His eternal rule and reign on earth. God in Christ had come to man. His coming affirmed the promise that all might be redeemed. In a sense Jesus announced the arrival of the kingdom of God on earth because no one else recognized it. He was born in obscurity to a virgin mother and raised by Joseph, who served as His earthly father. Even though the angels announced His birth, only shepherds heard the good news the night He was born (Luke 2:8-20). Later, much to the surprise and fear of King Herod who had no inkling of His birth, Magi from the East traveled to Jerusalem searching for Jesus. Even the Jewish scholars had to study the Scriptures to learn where the Messiah or King of God's people was born. Obviously, they had heard nothing about His birth (Matt. 2:1-6).

Imagine, the King of kings born in obscurity and poverty with those He came to redeem totally unaware of His birth. Yet the details of His birth are significant. What could be better than a ruler who completely identifies with those He came to rule? What could be more fitting than a leader, a sovereign, or a king with full understanding of his subjects? Jesus Christ gave up all the glory and honor of heaven to come to earth to be one of us. He is not a king who rules from above, but One who rules from among His people.

All that God can be is in Christ and all that man can be is in Him also.

41

He identifies with being human. He knows about rejection, grief, and struggles. He knows about feeling tired, frustrated, and angry, and about challenges to be understood and overcome. He knows about families and how they sometimes cannot relate or understand one another. He knows about death, and He knows about resurrection to new life. He knows about facing temptation. And He knows about the weight of our sin because He carried the weight of those sins and bore our punishment on the cross.

There are many reasons Jesus exercises the legitimate right to rule over all things in heaven and on earth, but perhaps most significant is the fact that He became a man. I do not know about you, but I would not for one moment consider worshiping a God who did not fully understand what life is like for me. I would not pray to any superior being if that being had not encountered the kinds of struggles I face daily. What assurance could you and I ever have of God's love if He had never known sorrow, pain, and death? Our King, Jesus Christ, came to us to meet our every need, and His coming signaled the beginning of God's reign on earth in the lives of persons who follow Him in faith.

Although Jesus was fully human, He was perfect in His humanness. His perfection gives us the assurance that what He says is true and what He does is right.

Have you considered what the coming of Jesus Christ really means to you? Have you considered that God's desire is to share an eternal relationship with you which He makes possible through Christ? The only way for that to occur was for Jesus Christ to come to earth, identify with us in life, and take our sins on Himself in death so that we could receive forgiveness and live within His kingdom forever.

Stop and Think! *Jesus understands our lives because He struggled with His humanity just like we do. What part of your life are you most glad Jesus understands? Why?*

_____

_____

_____

As a perfect man, Jesus was filled with the Holy Spirit and led by the Father. He never hurried, but He was always at the right place at the right time. He focused on what the Father wanted Him to do, but always had time for persons who needed Him. He is a model of one who submits to God's authority. We can observe how to live an abundant, purposeful life from Jesus because He came to earth and lived as we do.

How do you think of Christ today? Do you think of Him as the resurrected Lord and Savior in heaven with the Father? You are correct. The Bible tells us that at this very moment Jesus Christ does at least four things for us.

1. He prays and makes intercession for us and our needs.

"Christ Jesus is He who died, yes, rather who was raised, who is at the right hand of God, who also intercedes for us" (Rom. 8:34).

2. He is preparing a place for us to be with Him forever.

"In My Father's house are many dwelling places; if it were not so, I would have told you; for I go to prepare a place for you" (John 14:2-3).

3. He waits for the Father to tell Him to return to earth to consummate His kingdom.

"But of that day and hour no one knows, not even the angels of heaven, nor the Son, but the Father alone" (Matt. 24:36).

4. His greatest function is as mediator between God and man. Paul said, "For there is one God, and one mediator also between God and men, the man Christ Jesus" (1 Tim. 2:5). A mediator is one who stands between two parties yet exerts influence over both. He not only brings God and men together, but also He keeps them together by who He is and what He has done to bring salvation. Jesus is God—and He is man. He joins deity and humanity. As our Mediator and example, He influences us daily to live in righteousness and guides us in a proper relationship with the Father.

Following the arrest of John the Baptist, Jesus began to minister and teach in ways to prove that the kingdom of God had, in fact, come in power.

Have you ever thought about the nature of Christ in heaven? Jesus came to earth as God and took on an earthly body. He was conceived by a miracle of the Holy Spirit and born to Mary with a physical body like ours. However, He went back to heaven different from the way He came. He returned to heaven as the God-man with a resurrected body which He revealed to the disciples. He is still fully human and fully God in the Father's presence. And He identifys with us and our needs even though He is with the Father.

Although people hardly noticed Jesus' birth and the onset of His ministry, lack of response quickly changed. It is one thing to declare a fact; it is another to prove it day by day.

The Kingdom Ministry of Christ

The person of Jesus Christ cannot be fully separated from His ministry and teachings because who He is directly related to what He did and taught. For our purposes we will examine the different aspects of Jesus' ministry. At the chapter's conclusion we will endeavor to summarize and make application of truths.

Jesus' ministry can be divided into four parts. He did many things simultaneously, but He consistently ministered to persons in four ways.

First, He healed persons. This healing activity revealed His deity, changed the lives of persons to whom He ministered, and pointed men and women to God the Father. God has been healing persons since the beginning of time and history. However, Jesus' healing miracles affected those who witnessed them like no other healings.

Here's an example. Jesus healed a man who was blind from birth (John 9). As soon as the Pharisees saw the healed man, a controversy arose and they demanded to know how the man had regained his sight. He told them that Jesus had healed him. They argued that it was not possible because Jesus, in their opinion, was a sinner who did not observe the Sabbath, and sinners could not do such things.

The man stood by his testimony, however, and submitted a firm response.

Jesus' power displayed the presence of God's rule and reign on earth.

> *"Whether He is a sinner, I do not know; one thing I do know, that, whereas I was blind, now I see" (John 9:25).*

The Pharisees persisted in trying to get the man to change his story, but he would not. Finally, he lost patience with their examination of Him and added a powerful testimony to his already classic response.

> *"Since the beginning of time it has never been heard that anyone opened the eyes of a person born blind. If this man were not from God, He could do nothing" (John 9:32-33).*

Second, Jesus performed miracles. The miracles are meant to draw us to Him and give us understanding of who He is. It is a matter of revelation and faith. The revelation of God's power, authority, and control over nature and natural law calls us to believe in Him and come to Him. While it is not always easy to understand the miracles of God, they are for our benefit and God's own glory. Jesus said to Philip,

> *"Believe Me that I am in the Father, and the Father in Me; otherwise believe on account of the works themselves" (John 14:11).*

Jesus Christ could do what no one else had ever done. He could raise the dead, heal the sick and lame, calm winds and stormy seas, walk on water, and give sight to the blind. He never explained why bad things happened to the people He healed. He simply spoke to them, touched them, or commanded their infirmities to be removed. He never explained miracles except to point people to faith in the Father. It is unfortunate today that many believers seek miracles and the power to perform miracles apart from knowing God and doing His will. The kingdom of God focuses on Jesus Christ and entering into a relationship with Him which offers abundant and eternal life. Jesus did not heal every person who was sick in Judea in the first century. He did not walk on water everyday. He did not prevent storms from bringing wind and rain to the land. He did not raise from the dead every person who died during the years of His ministry. But when He did these things, His power revealed God's reign on earth.

Rewind. *Underline phrases in the preceding paragraph which describe the selective nature of Jesus' miracles and healing ministry. What does this selectivity reveal about the purpose of these acts?*

_____

_____

(If you need a hint, read the following paragraph.)

Jesus obeyed the will of God each day to introduce those watching to the Father in heaven. Each miracle revealed the kingdom of God by transforming the invisible, unknowable, and unthinkable into reality and fact and pointed individuals to the Father. Miracles still happen today. People are healed, sight is restored, and the dead are

"The result was that when Jesus had finished these words, the multitudes were amazed at His teaching; for He was teaching them as one having authority, and not as their scribes."

Matthew 7:28-29

brought back to life. Whenever and wherever we experience God at work, we observe miracles. Our response as Christians should be gratification and praise to Him for His power and work among us. Do not presume that God must or will do something for us if we have enough faith or if we do the right thing. Miracles are manifested according to the purposes of God and from His hand to fulfill those purposes.

Third, Jesus taught and preached with power and authority unlike anyone who had come before. He preached the message of the kingdom of God; it was the dominant theme for His entire ministry. Every great person who has ever made an impact in the world has been focused on a single idea. Jesus was focused on the kingdom of God. He preached it and taught it everywhere He went and to all who would listen. When He finished teaching and preaching the Sermon on the Mount, the crowd knew they had heard something special. Can you remember the last time you sat spellbound, listening to someone teach or preach from God's Word? You were moved, not because the person made it interesting, but because the Lord was speaking to you directly.

I remember having lunch with some friends and listening to a man speak about some of his life experiences. As he spoke I became conscious that God was using him in a powerful way to speak to me about some areas in my life. It was as if the Lord said, "Don't say anything; I want you to hear what this servant of mine is saying." When we left the restaurant that day, I was amazed at what I had learned.

Jesus taught about the kingdom of God—how to enter it, how to live in it, and how it will come in the future. We will study the Sermon on the Mount and its meaning for our lives in chapter 4, because it is the Scripture's most concise teaching on the kingdom.

Knowing that the kingdom of God was the focus of Jesus' teaching and preaching, it is surprising that more has not been written, preached, and taught about the subject. There are no major theologies written with the kingdom of God as the central focus. Recent book listings show only a few resources for believers to study. Why have we neglected this important and crucial study? This generation of Christians knows little about God's kingdom. A return to the teachings of Jesus will meet our need for learning about the kingdom of God.

How much of the kingdom of God do you know about and carry within your daily life? How would you describe your life in respect to

"Jesus said to the Pharisees who accused Him of being possessed, 'If I cast out demons by the finger of God, then the kingdom of God has come upon you.' "

Luke 11:20

Jesus' teachings in the Sermon on the Mount? Have you grown in your desire and ability to keep His commandments and to serve Him as He desires? We live in dark days—days of compromise and weakness in our churches, homes, marriages, and lives. Too often we accommodate our culture and ignore the kingdom to which we are called. Jesus taught with authority because what He believed is true and from the Father. We are His people, disciples, and followers; therefore, we must know His Word and the kingdom it reveals.

The fourth way Jesus ministered was through casting out demons. Many have tried to understand and explain demonic possession using scriptural references to it as psychological or physical illness. If the people had suffered such illnesses, Jesus would not have treated them as though demon possessed. The truth is they were possessed by demons and dominated by Satan until Jesus came to drive them out by His Word and authority. There is no greater evidence of God's kingdom coming to earth than in Jesus' ministry of exorcisms. When He entered a room, demons cried out in fear and for mercy. When He spoke, they were helpless against His Word. Jesus delivered persons from this enslavement as easily as He walked from place to place.

The ministry of Christ was founded upon these four pillars: healing, working miracles, teaching/preaching, and casting out demons.

Rewind. *Jesus' ministry was founded on four pillars. Label the pillars on the drawing below.*

Examples of the four pillars: healing, working miracles, preaching and teaching, and exorcisms (casting out demons) are found throughout the four Gospels.

Jesus proved repeatedly that God's reign on earth had begun and nothing could stop its power and authority. There was not a time of hesitation, a moment of doubt, or a day of discouragement in Jesus' life with respect to the kingdom of God. He preached its reality with conviction; He revealed it through miracles, healings, and exorcisms—and He never wavered. His confidence can be ours. Our understanding of reality comes from Jesus, His words, and His deeds. We must adjust our thinking to see in Him the kingdom of God and to live as He lived. The kingdom is the fundamental reality in our universe today and the driving force of history.

Jesus' Teaching and the Kingdom of God

Jesus was the Master Teacher and used many learning methods to communicate the message of God's kingdom to His hearers. He asked questions, illustrated, lectured, demonstrated, proclaimed, exhorted, rebuked, and listened to His followers as He taught them. In addition, He used healing, miracles, and exorcisms to strengthen His teaching. The focus of His teaching was the kingdom of heaven as God's good news (Matt. 4:17,23). We will focus our study on the Sermon on the Mount (Matt. 5–7) and the parables He used to speak about the kingdom.

The Sermon on the Mount is one of history's finest examples of literature. Its style is simple, but its message is powerful and dynamic. In it Jesus introduced the radical concept of linking a person's relationship with God to righteousness and the kingdom of heaven. The idea is that righteousness is necessary to enter the kingdom of heaven—"seek first His kingdom and His righteousness; and all these things shall be added to you" (Matt. 6:33).

This message was such a clear departure from anything the Jews had ever heard that its impact was revolutionary. Jesus preached the gospel, announcing the kingdom of God. His teaching focused on a person's standing before God in righteousness. (Righteousness means to be "straight" and not leaning.) Righteousness is a characteristic of God who is without sin, blemish, or fault. Jesus taught that anyone who was not righteous could not enter the kingdom. No one in the first century believed that a person could attain righteousness. Righteousness was an attribute reserved only for God. This message was radical and called for a true "repentance" or change of mind.

Jesus taught the necessity of a new life. This new life was not to be built upon fervor, religion, keeping the commandments, or emotion, but on the kingdom of God. Jesus' message of the kingdom was built,

Jesus said, "I say to you, that unless your righteousness surpasses that of the scribes and Pharisees, you shall not enter the kingdom of heaven."

Matthew 5:20

in summary, upon repentance (a complete change of mind) and righteousness (a complete change of life). Kingdom people are not like any other people. They do not live according to culture. They live in and have a relationship with God.

Rewind. *Fill in the blanks to complete simple definitions of repentance and righteousness.*

Repentance = a complete change of _____

Righteousness = a complete change of _____

In the exercise above you recalled that life in the kingdom of God is built upon repentance, which involves a complete change of mind, and righteousness, which means a complete change of life. The Sermon on the Mount reminds us that we are different from the pagan world and the nominally religious world around us. Our attitudes and lives express a completely different devotion and ethic from anyone else in the world. We have no power within ourselves to live a life of righteousness. We have no willpower to pursue the kingdom of God in its full meaning. But we receive from God all that we need and more than we ever will deserve. The Sermon on the Mount represents the power of Jesus' teaching to convict us of our deepest needs and drive us to God for help. The teaching of Jesus points to our failures and offers the resources we need to understand the kingdom of God and seek it with all our hearts.

Most of Jesus' parables explain some truth about the kingdom of God.

Jesus also taught kingdom truth through the use of parables. Jesus' parables are unique. There are examples of parables in other literature, but no one ever used them like Jesus. Parables are short stories which illustrate kingdom truths. We will not examine all of the parables, but some are important because of their specific meanings. Jesus' parables offer us understanding, encouragement, and strength for living. The following are examples of kingdom truths which Jesus taught in the parables.

• *The kingdom of God has come to provide persons the opportunity to return to the Lord.* Humankind, since Adam and Eve, has been separated from God in sin. Even Israel, God's chosen people, failed to keep their promises to obey and follow Him. In Luke 15 Jesus gives three parables (the lost sheep, the lost coins, and the lost son) to illustrate how the Father seeks us and waits for us to return to Him.

Jesus' message of good news (the gospel) and repentance called for a return to the Lord. The parable emphasizes the sinner's repentance and the joy it creates in heaven when a person returns to Him.

• *The kingdom of God is the moving force of history in our universe, and nothing can prevent its growth and development.* According to the parable of the seed (Mark 4:26-29), the kingdom of God produces growth "by itself" (v. 28), and no one quite understands how. The parables of the mustard seed and the leaven (yeast) illustrate that even though the kingdom appears small and is overlooked, it has an unpreventible force of growth and development. The rules of development for God's reign on earth are not governed by the laws of man. Men neither understand nor control the growth of God's kingdom.

• *The kingdom of God is always in competition with evil.* The Bible never explains the presence of evil except in the light of sin and rebellion toward God. Evil is acknowledged as anything which stands against God, His will, or His people. The parable of the wheat and tares (Matt. 13:24-30) reveals how Satan has planted his schemes and followers on earth as rivals to God's righteous servants. The battleground for this conflict is none other than the kingdom (13:41). Evil, however, grows to its own destruction while the kingdom of God is brought to fullness by the Son of man. At the end of history, Satan and his evil ones will be judged and cast away to hell and destruction.

• *History is moving toward a climax when the kingdom of God will be consummated (fully visible and operational) and evil finally will be destroyed.* The parable of the fig tree in Luke 21:29-36 indicates how quickly the day of the Lord will come. The parable of the 10 virgins in Matthew 25:1-13 reveals how the Lord's coming will find some persons prepared for Christ's return and others having made no preparation at all. Believers (the righteous) will be separated from unbelievers (the unrighteous) by judgment. Believers will reign with Christ and unbelievers will be cast away from God in hell forever.

• *The kingdom of God is life's greatest treasure, asset, or discovery.* The parable of the hidden treasure and the parable of the pearl of great price (Matt. 13:44-46) show how the kingdom of God, often overlooked, is priceless. Life's priority for believers is to seek and to find the kingdom. The parable of the talents (Matt. 25:14-30) reveals the manner in which Jesus gifts His children to serve Him in His kingdom and how He holds us accountable for the fruit He produces

The Sermon on the Mount and the parables are representative of Jesus' teachings concerning the kingdom of God.

in and through our lives. The results/fruit for which we are accountable to Jesus prove to be our greatest interests and endeavors.

Rewind. *Match the parable below with its corresponding truth about the kingdom of God.*

The lost sheep	*The kingdom is life's greatest discovery.*
The seed	*The kingdom is always competing with evil.*
The wheat and tares	*The kingdom is an opportunity to return to the Lord.*
The fig tree	*The kingdom is the predominant force in history.*
The hidden treasure	*The kingdom of God will be visibly consummated.*

"He delivered us from the domain of darkness, and transferred us to the kingdom of His beloved Son, in whom we have redemption, the forgiveness of sins."

Colossians 1:13-14

Let's review the teaching of these important parables. The parable of the lost sheep assures us that the kingdom offers us the opportunity to return to the Lord. The parable of the seed teaches that the kingdom is the predominant force in history. The parable of the wheat and tares reminds us that the kingdom is always competing with evil. The parable of the fig tree teaches that the kingdom will be visibly consummated. Finally, the parable of the hidden treasure teaches the truth that the kingdom is life's greatest discovery.

Actually all the teachings of Jesus relate to the kingdom and fall within three broad categories: (1) His summons to the kingdom of God through repentance and faith; (2) His call to living in the kingdom through discipleship; (3) The fulfillment of the kingdom which will occur at His return to earth.

The life of Christ, His ministry, and His teachings are God's revelation which brings about our redemption, gives us meaning in life, and leads us to eternity with confidence.

As you reflect upon the life, ministry, and teachings of Christ, are you aware of anything you lack in regard to the kingdom? Are your priorities those of a kingdom citizen? Do you follow Christ in a personal way, or do you tend to depend upon your religion to guide you? Is the kingdom of God your greatest treasure, asset, or discovery? Does your lifestyle set you apart from the world's culture?

Stop and Think! *These are probing questions! How will you adjust your lifestyle to better live as a kingdom citizen?*

_____

_____

_____

_____

The kingdom message is God's good news to us; it is an invitation to come home to Him where we belong. He created us for fellowship with Him, and we can share in it as we follow Christ to abundant life, joy, and peace. Paul's prayer of thanksgiving for the Colossians can be ours today. Remember that God has strengthened us with all power and qualified us to share in the inheritance of His saints. As believers we are in the domain of the Son of man, the Righteous One who rules and reigns by His life, death, and resurrection. We know that our sins are behind us, the kingdom is before us, and we possess our greatest treasure.

chapter 3

THE CALL TO THE KINGDOM

chapter 3

THE CALL TO THE KINGDOM

"Walk in a manner worthy of the God who calls you into His own kingdom and glory."

1 Thessalonians 2:12

Do you recall the well-known story of the Alamo? The small band of Texans were surrounded by the large and powerful army under the command of the famous Mexican general, Santa Ana. There seemed no hope for victory during the days leading up to the final assault. Led by legendary Americans such as Crockett, Bowie, and Travis, the men and women trapped in the small mission knew the danger that lay ahead. It is said that Colonel Travis summoned everyone to come together. Then he drew a line in the dirt. He asked that each person decide whether he wanted to stay and fight, or remain behind the line and leave. Every person, save one, stepped across the line determined to fight until the end.

These brave people will be remembered throughout American history because they were willing to answer the call, even though it guaranteed certain death. Not only does the kingdom of God call us to die to ourselves; but it also calls us to life in a new dimension. This call comes as the result of the dramatic action of God in His Son, Jesus Christ.

Jesus Christ brought the kingdom of God to earth in dramatic fashion. He is history's outstanding figure. Even those who reject Him and His gospel usually admit that He is unique, the most powerful person to ever live. Out of the life and ministry of Christ comes a call to each of us to return to our Creator and to a life of meaning and fulfillment. This call is a universal call and an individual call. God calls every person to salvation in Christ and fellowship with Him.

In this chapter we will discover how this call of God in Christ moves us to our significant place in the kingdom of God. God's call removes us from the destruction of sin and death to the power of life and righteousness through Him. We will see how sin destroys our humanity and mars the image and purposes of God in our lives. Ultimately we will see how Christ restores our lives and gives us our proper identity.

The Kingdom and Creation

To fully understand our identity and meaning in life we must return again to the time of creation. God created humankind in a unique, wondrous way for a special purpose. After the creation of all things, God saw that everything He made was good, adequate, and proper to complete His purposes. He then determined to create humankind as His final crowning, creative achievement.

> *"Then God said, 'Let Us make man in Our image, according to Our likeness; and let them rule over the fish of the sea and over the birds of the sky and over the cattle and over all the earth, and over every creeping thing that creeps on the earth.' And God created man in His own image, in the image of God He created him; male and female He created them" (Gen. 1:26).*

This significant verse identifies a number of important factors for us with respect to our identities under God.

First, we see that God Himself is a person who communicates (speaks), determines (wills), and purposes (does). The question of origins can only be addressed from two points: either we were created by a personal Creator, or we have come from an impersonal life-giving force. There really is no middle ground despite many attempts to find one.

The meaning of human life can never be derived from an impersonal life-giver. It defies logic that something which is not a person could create that which is a person.

Rewind. *Circle the number of the statement which best describes your view of creation.*

1. We were created gradually through evolution from other life forms.

2. We were created through evolution, with God as part of the process.

3. We were created by God, directly, and in God's image.

The Bible teaches that we are a special creation, that God created us directly and in God's image. If we were created by chance or by some impersonal life-giving force, then we have no reason to find significance in our lives or in our world. If, on the other hand, we were created by a personal God, we obtain significance, meaning, and identity from Him. On the one hand, we have the written

The kingdom of God manifests itself in His creative activity. He creates us, redeems us in Christ, and lives with us forever.

revelation of God (the Bible) which tells us of a divine Person who created man for His purposes. On the other hand, we have silence as to the origin of life. Even scientists shy away from offering solutions as to first cause. Science is only able to observe and state conclusions on what is observable. Creation is beyond the scope or power of scientific observation which must always begin somewhere after the first cause or creation-event.

Our lives are not determined by scientific theory, the latest psychological insight, or anything of the kind. Life can only be shaped formed, determined by the One who gives life and creates it with purpose and meaning. God our Father-Creator made us for Himself and His purposes.

Second, we see in this verse that we have been created with a uniqueness which other animals, plants, and matter in the universe do not possess. Humankind, created in the image and likeness of God, is given an assignment to rule over creation. According to Scripture, only man is created in God's image. Genesis 1:27 reveals the fact that man is God's final, crowning creation. Man gives perspective and meaning to all of creation. With man God achieved the purpose of creation.

We never can say of any human being that he or she is a mere animal. This concept destroys a person's significance and perpetuates the idea that human worth is functional. If a person is not deemed inherently valuable, then another person, government, or group can declare that person unwanted or expendable. Without significance, unborn children, the elderly, the poor, those who are helpless, members of racial minorities, or even unpopular religious persons can be exterminated.

All of God's activity eventually points to certain important truths. His redemptive purpose for our lives begins when He creates us. There are no accidental births to God. From our perspective, a child's conception can be a blessed event or a heartache, but God uses each birth to fulfill His purpose to redeem and bring that child into eternity with Him. The value of a child's life cannot be measured by his or her parents, environment, potential, or desirability. A person's worth is measured only by the Creator.

Third, humankind is created male and female, equal before God— but different. The image of God is not reflected separately by male and female as some have suggested. God does not have female and male characteristics. God's nature exists independently of sexuality.

For His purposes He made human beings male and female. This assigns significance to who we are, not only as members of the human race but also as individuals (male or female). To deny gender or to eliminate its significance to individuals is to deny God's purposes and to diminish a person's identity and meaning.

The biblical truth that humans are created in the image and likeness of God has been the subject of debate for centuries. But for our purposes in this study, we can list a number of human characteristics which reveal the image of God and set apart human beings from everything else in creation. Humans are rational; they can think about things outside their existence. They can reflect on reality. They even can think about abstract things. Humans display various and unique personalities; each person is different from every other. They are emotional and have feelings. They can communicate—verbally and nonverbally. They enter into relationships with others. They experience joy, love, sorrow, and other emotions. Humans possess a conscience, a sense of right and wrong which guides their behavior.

Humans reflect their Creator in His likeness and image. They are able to know Him, themselves, and others as well as communicate between themselves. They are linked to one another, responsible to God in a way unknown to other creatures. The image of God in man unlocks the purpose of his humanity in a unique way.

The truth that human persons are created in God's image sets them apart from everything else in creation.

Rewind. *List five characteristics of humankind which reveal the image of God.*

_____

_____

_____

_____

_____

The fact that humans are created in the image of God is a powerful truth. By way of review, it means that persons are rational, they have personalities, they are capable of emotion, they are able to relate to other persons, and they possess a conscience which gives them a sense of right and wrong.

Sin and the Image of God

My father told me a story that happened in his boyhood days which I have never forgotten. Near the end of the roaring 20's the sale of alcohol was legalized in the United States. This ended a period of prohibition during which alcohol could only be brewed and consumed illegally. On the day the ban was lifted, a neighbor passed by his father's house laughing and joking about his first legal drink. The neighbor chided my grandfather because he knew my grandfather felt strongly about the evils of alcohol. My father's words when he told this story remain in my mind: "He went to a bar for his first drink and never again drew a sober breath." In one day the man's life changed forever. Eventually he lost his wife, family, and self-respect. He never found his way back to being the man God intended him to be.

This story illustrates how sin can damage the life of any individual. Sin destroyed Adam and Eve's relationship with God. They were changed, separated from God, themselves, and each other. In reality, man's sin is his rebellion and determination to deny God as the source of meaning in life. With the fall of man into sin and the subsequent sin each of us has experienced, we have distorted the true image of God in our lives. This means that while we are created in His image, our beings are affected by sin so that we are cut off from God who is the source of all life, purpose, and meaning. In this sense we lose our identity because we are separated from God who is our life-giver; we are dead in our trespasses and sins. We do not lose rationality, emotion, communication, and knowledge, but we are unable to be at our best because sin distorts these functions from God's intended standard. The burden or plight we all share is that we are sinners, separated from God, from meaning, and from fulfillment. How can we overcome this terrible condition?

The kingdom of God brings with it a new identity—first with Christ, then with other believers. The kingdom person is made new because the old nature, the old man, the separated person is dead to God, His ways, His thoughts, and His works.

The Incarnation of Christ

Scripture makes it clear that individuals have no hope in their

We are not what God intended, and in our sins, we cannot realize our full potential as human beings.

Jesus Christ is the Redeemer through whom all God's purposes in creation are brought to completion.

condition of sinfulness. There is nothing a person can do, think, or say that triumphs over the effects of sin. The total absence of any resources to pay for sin's devastating effects on our lives is indeed the plight of man. The Old Testament teaches this not only in the many declarations of man as a sinner in need of salvation, but also in Israel's total failure to keep her covenant with God. God made the covenant and provided His strength to keep Israel in relationship with Him. Unfortunately, time after time Israel moved away from God, rebelled against God, and resisted neither sin nor idolatry. Neither the law, the priests, the kings, nor the prophets prevented Israel from rejecting God. The plight of man is understandable in ignorant pagans or immoral persons, but Isaiah declares, "My name is continually blasphemed all day long" (Isa. 52:5).

Stop and Think! *Define or describe the "plight of man" in your own words.*

_____

_____

_____

_____

_____

_____

"He is the image of the invisible God, the first-born of all creation. For by Him all things were created, both in the heavens and on earth, visible and invisible ... all things have been created by Him and for Him. And He is before all things, and in Him all things hold together."

Colossians 1:15-17

If God's own chosen nation could not keep the covenant because of sin, then no one else could either. It would take God's own action. It would require a total work of grace, not anything man could provide for himself. God would have to remove man's sin. He would do this in dramatic fashion by actually becoming a man—Jesus Christ, Son of God and Son of man—fully God and fully man. He revealed the transformation of a redeemed man. In Christ, we see a model for daily living. We also see what human nature will be when Jesus Christ returns to establish His kingdom on earth.

Jesus, the Son of God, is the very expression of God's image in human form. He is also the expression of God's will and power in

In Jesus we have the restoration of God's plans, purposes, and promises to His people.

creation because He created all things and keeps all things together.

In summary, we see that man is God's creature, made in His image. Man's sin has distorted that image and separated man from God. Jesus Christ is the fulfillment of what God intended man to be when He created him. What we have lost in sin, Jesus Christ came to earth to restore. Jesus is truly God. He fulfills God's redemptive mission on earth. He is a bridge between God and man.

Our Identity in Christ

The work of Christ restores what we lost to sin. Through Him we have a new meaning, purpose, and identity. What we saw lost in the Old Testament is regained in the New Testament. God planned for Israel to be His chosen nation, to become a kingdom of priests unto Him (Ex. 19:6). Paul declares: "You have died and your life is hidden with Christ in God. When Christ, who is our life, is revealed, then you also will be revealed with Him in glory" (Col. 3:3-4).

With words echoing the content of Exodus, Peter declared that we have a new identity as the people of God. In 1 Peter 2:4-10, he gave us the identity of kingdom citizens, an identity with Christ.

Let's notice how Jesus Christ is described in these verses. He is:

- A living stone
- Rejected by men
- Choice and precious in the sight of God
- Rejected
- Cornerstone
- Stone of stumbling and a rock of offense.

The call to the kingdom of God is a call to take advantage of what God offers to us in Christ and to become what we were created to be.

Stop and Think! *Read 1 Peter 2:4-10 in your Bible. Underline words or phrases which describe Jesus Christ. Write the most interesting or meaningful phrase in the space that follows.*

_____

_____

_____

_____

Now notice what Peter says about our identity with Jesus. We are:

- Living stones
- A spiritual house for a holy priesthood
- A chosen race
- A royal priesthood
- A holy nation
- A people for God's own possession
- The people of God

Stop and Think! *Read 1 Peter 2:4-10 again. This time, underline the words or phrases which describe your identity in Christ. Write the most interesting or meaningful phrase in the space below.*

_____

_____

_____

"The stone which the builders rejected has become the chief corner stone."

Psalm 118:22

Our identity in Christ is related to what He accomplished for us. He is a living stone. Like the chief stone in a first-century building which must hold the weight and give shape to a structure, Jesus is our source for salvation. The Father placed upon Him the entire weight of His redemptive plan for our salvation. He is the most important stone in the structure which God Himself is building. He is choice and precious in the sight of God. Our identity is taken from the cornerstone. We also are "living stones ... being built up as a spiritual house for a holy priesthood" (1 Pet. 2:5). Jesus Christ is the cornerstone of God's work in the world, and we are "little" or small stones built upon Him. What He is, we are. What He does, we do. What He purposes, we accomplish. We are a part of the "spiritual house" and "holy priesthood" because of our relationship with Him.

Jesus Christ was rejected and despised. He was an offense to the world He came to save, but the Father was pleased to send Him and use Him to bring redemption to earth. He did not come as God-man to complete creation, which was already "very good," according to Genesis 1:31. Rather, He came to recreate, to restore, and to reconcile us to the Father. We find identity with Him and in Him.

Peter declares, "Once you were not a people, but now you are the people of God; you had not received mercy, but now you have

We find the image and likeness of God fully displayed in Christ and fully available to us in Him.

"You are a chosen race, a royal priesthood, a holy nation, a people for God's own possession, that you may proclaim the excellencies of Him who has called you out of darkness into His marvelous light."

1 Peter 2:9

received mercy" (1 Pet. 2:10). Jesus Christ and our relationship with Him is what makes the difference and gives us this identity. Peter mentions four distinguishing characteristics of God's people in verse 9. Notice that each of these relates to the person or being and not to the actions of that person or being. We must be something before God can do anything through us. Christians receive their identity and worth from who they are, not what they do or accomplish. It is not our knowledge, intellect, accomplishments, or abilities, but our relationship with the Lord which makes us who we are. Presented in 1 Peter 2:9 are the four identifying marks we have in Christ.

• *We are called a "chosen race."* The Old Testament is full of references to Israel as the people of God being especially chosen for His purposes and glory. Moses reminded the people in Deuteronomy 10:14-15 that all things in the heavens and earth belong to the Lord: "Yet on your fathers did the Lord set His affection to love them, and He chose their descendants after them, even you above all peoples, as it is this day."

Notice how the choosing of believers parallels the choosing and electing of God's Son, Jesus Christ. What is true about His election is true of ours because God "chose us in Him before the foundation of the world, that we should be holy and blameless before Him" (Eph. 1:4). Jesus Christ is God's elect One. We share this identity with Him through grace and faith. Our identity, then, is a result of our relationship with Christ and our sharing His nature. His life is ours and His character is ours. We are declared righteous by God. We live by the working of the Holy Spirit within our lives.

Can you fully imagine the impact that being part of a "chosen race" has on your life? He chose you just like He chose Israel—for His own reasons, according to His own purposes. He chose Israel as His new people in Christ to use in His kingdom work. I wonder how many believers and how many churches truly feel special today because God has chosen them? Do you try to live in a way to impress God with your life and devotion to Him, or do you live in devotion to Him because He has chosen you? Are you trying to thank Him for salvation with your good works, or do you serve Him because of who you are in Christ?

No matter how sinful your past might have been, or how unworthy you are, His choosing you changes everything. He chose to bring you into a personal relationship with Him and to use you to accomplish His purposes. The longer you live in Christ, the more like Christ you become. This truth reveals a clear understanding of our identity in Christ Jesus. We are chosen and set apart for the Father.

Rewind. *Mark the following statements T (true) or F (false).*
___ *The record of God's pattern of having a special "chosen" people began in the Old Testament.*
___ *God's choice of you as His child involved the forgiveness of your sin through the sacrifice of Christ.*
___ *God chose you, in Christ, before the creation of the world.*

I am sure you marked "true" for all three of the above statements.

• *We are a "royal priesthood."* Priests unto God? We may be inclined to say, "No way!" That we are called priests is truly amazing. We came to Christ dead in our trespasses and sins. Paul said that apart from Christ, we are dominated by the world, Satan, and our own lusts of the flesh and mind (Eph. 2). But God intervened and we were changed by grace. We became a kingdom, priests unto God. This truth is echoed throughout Scripture.

> *"You will be called the priests of the Lord;*
> *You will be spoken of as ministers of our God" (Isa. 61:6).*
> *"He has made us to be a kingdom, priests to His God and Father" (Rev. 1:6).*

> *"Thou hast made them to be a kingdom and priests to our God; and they will reign upon the earth" (Rev. 5:10).*

Notice that we are a corporate priesthood, not individual priests. The priesthood of the believer is always in the context of believers together or collectively. And what makes us priests? What does a priest do? We offer something to the Lord in the kingdom of God. We come before Him and give Him something that He desires and commands. What could you offer the Father today that He needs or does not have? He owns all things, controls all things, and brings all things to completion. Could you offer some thought or concept which He has not already considered? Could you build something He could not build or write something He would find unique?

God does not call upon us to offer these things. He asks us to offer only one thing—our lives. In Romans 12:1-2 the Lord asks us to give

We must come to grips with the fact that before the foundation of the world God had us in mind, not only to create us and save us but also to use us in His kingdom.

63

"I urge you therefore, brethren, by the mercies of God, to present your bodies a living and holy sacrifice, acceptable to God, which is your spiritual service of worship. And do not be conformed to this world, but be transformed by the renewing of your mind, that you may prove what the will of God is, that which is good and acceptable and perfect."

Romans 12:1-2

ourselves as living sacrifices. This is not in order for Him to consume us, but for Him to empower us and to use us for His purposes. We are priests who belong to the King, and our task is to serve Him and His kingdom purposes.

Have you ever tried to buy a gift for a person who has everything? It's a difficult task because such people appear to be without need or desire of any kind. Every tangible gift idea you consider, they already possess. Or, items you believe would be enjoyable may not fit their personality. Clothes are not a good idea because they already wear the best brands. I once was pastor to a man who fit this description. He was a generous, wealthy, self-sufficient individual. He seemed to want nothing. One year for his birthday I invited him to lunch and insisted on paying before we arrived at the restaurant. He, of course, refused. I surprised him, when during lunch, I retrieved a card on which I had listed 10 questions about his childhood, parents, favorite people, dreams, and special times in his long life. He was delighted to talk about himself at my request. I could not give him a material gift, but I gave my time and my interest.

God asks us to come to Him and offer ourselves. It is what He requires, and it is all that He wants. It is acceptable and pleasing to Him, and it is reasonable in our service of worship to Him. We might expect Him to expect more from us, but this is all that He desires. Being priests before the Lord and belonging to His kingdom are vital parts of our identity. Together we are priests before the Lord. Collectively we offer to Him the worship of our lives.

Let's examine the nature of belonging to a group of persons who collectively live and minister the purposes of God—a church. Each of us has a vital function in its life, history, and health. We are members of the church which spans time and history and includes the faithful men and women who have gone before us, as well as those who now love the Lord. It reaches to the future with the ministry and lives of those who are yet to come. As individuals we join local churches. These local congregations exist across the world in every nation, tribe, and culture. As believers we are one in Christ and many in the Lord at the same time. The whole body of Christ is included when we say we are "in" Christ. The local expression of Christ's body is represented when we give the location of the fellowship of believers with whom we worship and serve daily. We are priests offering ourselves to God through Christ, and our lives are forever characterized by this relationship and service.

As priests we can offer:

1. Our lives as fully acceptable to Him.
   (Rom. 12:1)

2. Our service as a sacrifice to Christ.
   (Phil. 2:17)

3. Our material substance as an acceptable sacrifice.
   (Phil. 4:18)

4. Our praise as a sacrifice of thanksgiving.
   (Heb. 13:15)

5. Our good works as a sacrifice of sharing.
   (Heb. 13:16).

Rewind. *Circle the word which makes each sentence true.*

1. (All, Some) believers in Jesus Christ are priests.

2. Believers must offer (sacrifices, themselves) to God as their priestly service.

3. Priestly service is offered (collectively, individually) to God through the church.

The wonderful truth is that all believers are priests who offer themselves to God. Our priestly service involves the body of Christ; therefore, we offer that service collectively as a part of His church.

Holy means to be completely focused on the Father and His purposes, completely focused on Christ and His kingdom, and completely focused on the Holy Spirit empowering us to do kingdom work.

• *We are a "holy nation."* Once again the imagery of a people set apart and dedicated to God for His purposes is traced through the Old Testament.

> *"You shall be to Me ... a holy nation" (Ex. 19:6).*

> *"You are a holy people to the Lord your God" (Deut. 7:6).*

> *"Israel was holy to the Lord,*
> *The first of His harvest" (Jer. 2:3).*

We are each chosen by the Father to be "holy and blameless" (Eph. 1:4). Paul expanded this truth to say that the church as the bride of Christ is loved, sanctified, and cleansed by Him in order that He might present her "holy and blameless" (Eph. 5:27). Again in Colossians 1:22 Paul taught that Christ reconciled us to God that we might be holy and blameless. The word *blameless* speaks to our complete forgiveness and restoration unto the Father through Christ. The word *holy* means *set aside for His purposes.*

God intends to accomplish His purposes of salvation in all the earth. He creates persons each day He intends to redeem. He sets us apart for His service and the work of evangelism and discipleship throughout the world. He does this today just as long ago He declared the Israelites a holy people (Ex. 19:6). Notice Moses' explanation of this identity:

> *"The Lord did not set His love on you nor choose you*
> *because you were more in number than any of the peoples,*
> *for you were the fewest of all peoples, but because the Lord*
> *loved you" (Deut. 7:6-8).*

Our identity as kingdom people comes from the understanding that we have been set apart not for our ability, righteousness, or strength, but for the purposes and works of God.

Whatever *holy* might mean to us from our background and understanding, it must mean that God has separated us from all that we were. We can never again mix loyalties between what we are in Christ and what we were before Christ. No one can serve God and mammon at the same time; nor can we love the kingdom and the world. We cannot live with mixed motives, lifestyles, and desires. The things of God are a way of life to those who are in the kingdom. It is our identity as believers to be set apart for Him and His purposes, and our personal agendas are always subject to the will of God.

Holy does not mean *sinless, perfect,* and *never failing. Holy* does imply moral purity as a result of our relationship with God. It is an identity which comes from God's grace and work in our lives.

Stop and Think! *Since holiness means set aside for God's purposes, what in your life is evidence of your holiness?*

_____

_____

What in your life hinders evidences of holiness? Ask God now to help you change those attitudes or actions.

_____

_____

_____

_____

- *We are "a people for God's own possession."* The *King James Version* translates this phrase "a peculiar people." Believers are peculiar in the truest sense of the word. Why? Because we are created in His image, we are the crown of creation, and He has bestowed upon us a higher status than any other creation.

Angels are messengers and servants of God who serve His purposes. The Old Testament presents man's placement as just below the angels. In the New Testament, however, the position of a believer and an angel are reversed. Peter said in 1 Peter 1:10-12 that the salvation we receive in Christ and which the prophets foretold is something that angels long to look into (v. 12). Salvation brings a significance to one's life which angels and other heavenly beings do not experience. Before Christ, persons are lower than angels because angels serve God and have no need for God's law as humans do. But in Christ persons are redeemed from the law's curse by God's grace and receive a status in Christ as priests to reign with Him (Rev. 20:6).

In Christ, God has condemned our sins forever on the cross. Through His mercy He has forgiven and pardoned us. By His grace we are saved, sealed with His Holy Spirit, and receive an inheritance which can never be destroyed or taken from us. Christ sees Himself in us as a father recognizes himself in one of his children.

The psalmist says,

"The Lord loves the righteous" (Ps. 146:8);

"The Lord takes pleasure in His people" (Ps. 149:4).

Many years ago my wife arranged a visit to a museum to view some Fabergé eggs. I confess I had never heard of Fabergé eggs, and

"When I consider thy heavens, the work of thy fingers, the moon and the stars, which thou hast ordained; What is man, that thou art mindful of him? and the son of man, that thou visitest him? For thou hast made him a little lower than the angels, and hast crowned him with glory and honour."

Psalm 8:3-5, KJV

I wondered why she was so excited about looking at eggs when I wanted to play my usual Monday round of golf. Then I considered that because her father was a chicken farmer in Mississippi, perhaps she missed seeing eggs! To satisfy her and my own curiosity, we went to the museum. I experienced one of the nicest surprises of my life. For those of you who do not know, a Fabergé egg is a priceless work of art. They are decorated with precious stones and gems, and the designs create beautiful configurations. Crystal eggs of the highest quality in craftsmanship and value, Fabergé eggs are a treasure to behold!

If we owned one of those eggs, how do you think we might care for it? We would be careful not to damage it, and we might not allow anyone to handle it. It would be a priceless possession to us. This was Peter's idea when he wrote that we are a people of God's own possession. We are priceless to Him, peculiar to Him, and precious like Jesus is precious to God.

Of all God's creations, those who are in Christ are the most valuable to Him. Nothing in heaven or earth matches the value which God placed in you when He gave you the gift of salvation. What He sees in you, even at your worst, is exactly what He sees when He looks to His right in heaven and sees Jesus Christ. We have His forgiveness of sins and His righteousness.

It is important to know who we really are because it affects the way we understand ourselves and the way we live. We belong to the Lord, and the meaning, fulfillment, and pleasure we have in this life is a result of our relationship with Him. We are His treasure and priceless possession. Remember this fact when you are discouraged, treated unfairly by others, and tempted by Satan. We tend to believe what others say about us or the cultural messages given off about our inadequacies. In Colossians, chapter 2, Paul reminded us, "In Him [Jesus] all the fulness of Deity dwells in bodily form, and in Him you have been made complete, and He is the head over all rule and authority" (9-10).

Persons who respond to God's grace by trusting Christ are given immeasurable standing and completeness.

In Jesus Christ we lack nothing. There is nothing more to add, take away, or possess. Jesus is complete, and in Him we are complete. The recognition of our identity in Christ is essential to living a purposeful life and joining God in fulfilling His purposes to redeem our world. Our calling from Him brings an identity of security and significance which provides all that we need to do and be what God desires.

Rewind. *Re-read this section on being a people of God's own possession. List words or phrases which describe your value or uniqueness to God.*

_____

_____

_____

_____

You are His priceless possession, and He is not going to let anything happen to you which destroys you and removes you from His presence. You are His greatest treasure.

You would be correct to identify many wonderful facts that describe our value and uniqueness to God. We are the crown of His creative purpose, made in His image. Our sins have been forgiven. We have been sealed by His Holy Spirit. We have an inheritance in Him. We are complete in Christ. All of this—and more,—gives us as believers identity and security.

• *We have this identity (chosen race, royal priesthood, holy nation, God's own possession) for a reason, and that reason is to proclaim God's excellencies to our world.* This truth speaks directly to our calling in Christ and our fulfilling God's purposes in life. We are saved from sin to serve the Lord. We are called to accomplish this task. Our salvation is a calling, our lives and lifestyles are a calling, and our service to the Lord is a divine calling to each believer personally and directly from the Lord. We have been chosen to:

1. Live by God's choosing.
2. Be saved in Christ by God's grace.
3. Share the life of Christ.
4. Live a full, purposeful, and eternal life.
5. Serve the Lord to accomplish His purposes.

The call to the kingdom of God is a person's ultimate experience because it brings God's will into our lives and changes everything about us. Once we had no identity, no future, no purpose in life or standing before God, but now by God's mercy we possess all of these. God has worked in our lives to make us different and has filled us with the meaning of His purposes.

How many persons do you know who profess to be believers but live unhappy lives? How many believers do you know who live out the identity of one who has been called by God? Do you think your life and the lives of most Christians you know are identified by the realities of God's Word when it declares we are chosen, holy people? Israel's identity came from God and His covenant. Israel had nothing to offer the world—no power, no culture, no social advancements. The people of God were enslaved without hope of escaping bondage to Pharaoh.

This is our testimony as well. We are not better than others in our world. We are not smarter, more powerful, or more appealing than any person outside of Christ. We have nothing to offer a holy, sovereign, triune God. There is nothing we can do for Him that He cannot do Himself. But we are in Christ by His grace and therefore have a new identity. We are significant in Christ and our lives are, in fact, a calling to something beyond ourselves. Our task is to proclaim the excellencies of the God who calls us and makes us who we are. This important fact determines the significance in our lives as believers. We find our significance in our call from God and from the relationship we share with Him. To enter into the presence of the God of the universe and the Creator and Redeemer of our lives is to acknowledge who we are in the most significant way possible. We are called to enter His presence and worship Him with thanksgiving and praise. We are called to offer the best of all that He has given us. We are called to abide with Him and talk to Him in prayer. We are called to make our requests known to Him and to petition Him as often as we like. We are called to seek Him with all our hearts and souls with the promise that when we do, we will find Him.

We are called to be and become something that is impossible apart from Christ—something that far exceeds what any man or woman is capable of apart from God's grace.

Believers who seek to know the Lord find the significance that everyone hopes for but few seem to find. Moses said it clearly:

> *"You will seek the Lord your God, and you will find Him if you search for Him with all your heart and all your soul"* (Deut. 4:29).

> *"And now, Israel, what does the Lord your God require from you, but to fear the Lord your God, to walk in all His ways and love Him, and to serve the Lord your God with all your heart and with all your soul, and to keep the Lord's commandments and His statues which I am commanding you today for your good?"* (Deut. 10:12-13).

David joined Moses in words of admonition to Solomon, "If you seek Him, He will let you find Him; but if you forsake Him, He will reject you forever" (1 Chron. 28:9).

Jeremiah records the promise of God: " 'For I know the plans that I have for you,' declares the Lord, 'plans for welfare and not for calamity to give you a future and a hope. Then you will call upon Me and come and pray to Me, and I will listen to you. And you will seek Me and find Me, when you search for Me with all your heart' " (Jer. 29:11-13).

Jesus completes the admonition in the Sermon on the Mount, "Ask, and it shall be given to you; seek, and you shall find; knock, and it shall be opened to you" (Matt. 7:7).

Do you notice a standing invitation? We have the privilege of coming to the God of the universe. We can enter His presence whenever we choose and pursue a deep relationship with Him. There are no limits on knowing God. We cannot know everything about Him, but we can know Him to the fullest extent of our capabilities. Also, when we know God we learn more about His truth, and we receive understanding of things far beyond our present knowledge.

The key is seeking the Lord with all of your heart. A passion for God, to know Him, and to be with Him results in knowledge of Him, ourselves, and of His purposes. The important thing is to have the right heart which leads to the right experience. Would you like to acquire more knowledge of God, more peace of mind, and more meaning in life? It is available to you because of who you are. You are a child of God, choice and precious to Him, and in line to receive all His blessings.

In kingdom living, a right heart leads to the right experience.

Stop and Think! *Shade in this heart to symbolize your devotion to Jesus Christ at this time in your life.*

What is keeping you from wholehearted devotion to the Lord and what will you do about it?

_____

_____

_____

_____

There is one surprising dimension to these truths. Although Jesus accomplished everything we need to experience a proper relationship with God, we still encounter trials, sins, and failures in our lives. There is an ongoing struggle between the knowledge of our righteousness before God and the acute awareness that we are not yet all that we can be. Paul addressed this in the Book of Colossians. We read in Colossians 1:28 that Paul's goal was to present believers complete in Christ. In other words, we are what we are becoming. This is a simple truth that is often overlooked by believers.

In Christ, we are what we are becoming.

We struggle with the truths of God and with the growing pains of Christian living. We know that our identity in Christ provides eternal salvation, the presence of the Holy Spirit in our lives, and our place in the family of God on earth. We have the right and obligation to live out this life and this identity to the fullest extent possible. We must live with a mind-set to serve the Lord and to allow Him to accomplish His purposes in our world. If we live in any other manner, we are not true to our identity and we will never find the true meaning in life.

Scripture presents a different view of ourselves than we often hold when life is tough and our sins are constantly before us. The Bible describes us as righteous in Christ and inheritors of the kingdom.

The Bible uses words like these to describe the real you: *saint, joint-heir, child, holy one, friend, disciple, son, beloved of God, chosen, elect, predestined, fellow-citizen, partaker of the divine nature, Christian, adopted, brother, sister, priest, child of light, living stone, chosen, royal priest, holy nation, person of God's own possession.*

Each day we live, Jesus Christ reigns in our hearts and displays Himself in, through, and around us. Our identity as kingdom saints makes an enormous difference in the way we see ourselves and the way we live to accomplish His purposes in the world.

Chapter 4

LIVING IN THE KINGDOM
OF GOD

Chapter 4

LIVING IN THE KINGDOM OF GOD

"Seek first His kingdom and His righteousness; and all these things shall be added to you."

Matthew 6:33

I heard about a man who had the strange experience of discovering who he really was. He was given up by his parents during World War II to protect him from the concentration camps in Eastern Europe where his parents were sent to their deaths. He grew up knowing he was adopted, but without any information about his birth parents. One day three persons came to his home and disclosed his Jewish identity and the story of his parents' heroic decision to save him from death. He was deeply shaken by this new knowledge and immediately experienced an identity crisis. How should he feel? Should he act differently? Should he become a practicing Jew? These questions provoked a major change in his lifestyle.

In this chapter we will learn how God calls us to Himself and builds character within our lives so that we may join Him to complete His redemptive purposes in the world. We will see the relationship between being complete in Christ and serving the Lord. We will understand more clearly the relationship between what we are and what we do for Christ.

Our identity as believers demands that we live differently. In Christ we receive all the benefits of adoption into the family of God, but we cannot escape our real identity and purpose in living as kingdom citizens. Out of our call to God through Christ comes a call to become like Him in all aspects of our lives. We are called by a holy God to become holy unto Him. To be holy means to be set apart for God and His purposes, and it means to live in such a manner as to reflect this purpose in our lives. Our character comes directly out of our call to the kingdom of God. Character is also a reflection of the work of the Holy Spirit in our lives. Who we are determines how we live and express our faith in daily living.

Righteousness is the best expression of Christian character and virtue. You will remember from an earlier definition that at its root it means *straight* or *not leaning or crooked in any respect*. This is certainly a true description of the believer. In Christ there is nothing that is or can be wrong with us. We are forgiven, restored to fellowship with God, redeemed from the penalty of our sins, and complete in Christ. But for the believer, righteousness means something more. It means different—different from the world, from society, and from those outside of Christ.

The Lord made it clear to Moses and the Israelites that true righteousness must be reflected in life when He said:

> " 'You shall not do what is done in the land of Egypt where you lived, nor are you to do what is done in the land of Canaan where I am bringing you; you shall not walk in their statutes. You are to perform My judgments and keep My statutes, to live in accord with them; I am the Lord your God' " (Lev. 18:3-4).

When we enter the kingdom of God we enter a higher realm. Thus, we possess a different character and lifestyle. Righteousness ultimately means to be like Christ.

Rewind. *Mark the following statements T (true) or F (false).*

___ *The root meaning of righteous is straight or not leaning or crooked in any way.*

___ *For the believer, to be righteous means to be different from the world.*

___ *Righteousness ultimately means to be like Christ.*

All of the statements above are true. God is not like any of the other gods people may choose to worship. He is different, and in our relationship with Him we are different. Let's look at how this difference affects our lives and influences our development as believers.

We are called to an eternal relationship with Him, but we are also called to serve His purposes.

Out of character comes the ability to work for the Lord. We are called to serve the Lord with the gifts we have been given. God is on mission in our world, redeeming those He has created for His own purposes and glory. We each have been fitted for a unique task. Have you ever noticed how many different things people in the Bible did for the Lord?

- Adam named the animals God created.
- Noah built the ark.
- Moses led the Israelites out of Egypt.
- Joshua fought God's enemies in the promised land.
- The judges delivered Israel in terrible times.
- The kings ruled over the nations of Judah and Israel.
- The prophets spoke God's Word.
- The priests served the Lord in the temple.
- The disciples learned from Jesus.
- The apostles evangelized persons and built churches.
- The biblical authors recorded God's message.

The Lord calls believers to a personal relationship with Him, provides the Holy Spirit to develop His character within, and invites them to be used for His purposes. Paul reminded Titus of this when He said that Jesus Christ "gave Himself for us, that He might redeem us from every lawless deed and purify for Himself a people for His own possession, zealous for good deeds" (Titus 2:14). Jesus willingly died on the cross to purify us by the cleansing of His blood. That sacrifice identified believers as God's choice possessions. The sacrifice also enabled us to understand exactly what God did for us in Christ, how we are to live as Christians, and what we are to accomplish through our good deeds. Although many persons confuse activity with godliness and accomplishment with service, our relationship with Christ is the foundation of work within the kingdom of God. The kingdom of God, however, is not built like anything else. It is the work of a sovereign God who moves and shapes history according to His divine will and plan.

"For I say unto you, that unless your righteousness surpasses that of the scribes and Pharisees, you shall not enter the kingdom of heaven."

Matthew 5:20

Rewind. *Match the phrase on the left with the phrase on the right which best completes the sentence.*

	is built by hard-working, industrious Christians.
The kingdom of God	*depends on God but is built by Christians.*
	is built by God according to His will and plan.

76

The important truth is that the kingdom of God is built only by God according to His divine plan.

Righteousness and the Kingdom of God

The Bible is the believer's handbook for Christian living, and the Sermon on the Mount is Scripture's most concise teaching on living in the kingdom of God. As revealed in these verses, the kingdom of God is combined with righteousness in a way which is plain and powerful. To enter the kingdom of God is to become righteous through Christ and to pursue righteousness in our daily lives. God's character is righteousness, and we share that character, expressed through Jesus Christ, when we enter into relationship with Him.

To enter the kingdom of God is to become righteous and to pursue righteousness in our lives daily.

> *Pharaoh sent for Moses and Aaron, and said to them, "I have sinned this time; the Lord is the righteous one, and I and my people are the wicked ones" (Ex. 9:27).*

> *"O Lord God of Israel, Thou art righteous" (Ezra 9:15).*

> *"Behold the days are coming," declares the Lord,*
> *"When I shall raise up for David a righteous Branch;*
> *And He will reign as king and act wisely*
> *And do justice and righteousness in the land" (Jer. 23:5).*

> *" 'In those days and at that time I will cause a righteous Branch of David to spring forth; and He shall execute justice and righteousness on the earth' " (Jer. 33:15).*

> *By His knowledge the Righteous One,*
> *My Servant, will justify the many,*
> *As He will bear their iniquities (Isa. 53:11).*

> *"If anyone sins, we have an Advocate with the Father, Jesus Christ the righteous" (1 John 2:1).*

> *I heard the angel of the waters saying, "Righteous art Thou, who art and who wast, O Holy One, because Thou didst judge these things" (Rev. 16: 5).*

Jesus Christ is called righteous because His whole nature and life

We take our complete identity from Jesus Christ who in Scripture is revealed as righteous.

conforms perfectly to the will of God. Those who are "right," and "straight," and "perfect" conform to the will of God in their inward lives as well as their outward lifestyles.

The Sermon on the Mount (Matt. 5–7) combines the kingdom of God with righteousness. God's kingdom has come in Jesus Christ and is present in our world today. God has launched in these final days a powerful force of judgment and redemption. Entrance into this kingdom comes solely by faith in Christ and results in righteousness in the life of the believer. The kingdom of God cannot be separated from righteousness. Righteousness is a gift from God, in Christ, through the Holy Spirit.

Let's take a brief look at the Sermon on the Mount and see how righteousness and the kingdom of God relate to each other. Matthew 5:3-12 (often called the Beatitudes) points the way to true fulfillment in life. The Beatitudes are Christ's requirements for kingdom citizens. Paul lists nine expressions of the fruit of the Spirit in Galatians 5:22-23. The fruit of the Spirit and the eight Beatitudes describe the qualities which characterize believers.

Stop and Think! *Read Galatians 5:22-23. List the nine manifestations of the fruit of the Spirit.*

_____

_____

_____

_____

_____

_____

_____

The kingdom of God is present in the hearts of true believers. It is present in the church among those who have totally submitted their lives to Christ. The following qualities are the sequential outcome of the work of the Holy Spirit within a person's life who truly trusts in and completely follows Jesus.

The upward progression begins with a person who comes to understand his plight in spiritual poverty before the Lord. "Blessed are the poor in spirit, for theirs is the kingdom of heaven" (Matt. 5:3). This does not refer to financial poverty, but the poverty of soul which each of us has in our sinful condition. Because we are sinners by nature and by choice, spiritual poverty rules our lives. We cannot be holy like God because we are sinful like Adam. We cannot be righteous because we have missed the mark of God's glory set for us in creation and coming to bear upon us from the day of our birth. God does not relax the standards because we fall short of them.

As we come to the Father in Christ and take our identity from Him, we become acutely aware of who He is and who we are.

Spiritual poverty is the first step to righteousness. Persons who come to understand their spiritual poverty see themselves as God sees them—as they really are. They have no resources, nothing to rely upon to give purpose to life and assurance beyond death. They are undone and wounded in spirit. God's people always come to Him in spiritual poverty because there is no other way. We can identify with the saints of the Bible when they declare:

- David: *"Against Thee, Thee only, have I sinned,*
        And done what is evil in Thy sight" (Ps. 51:4)

- Nehemiah: *"We have sinned against Thee; I and my father's*
        house have sinned" (Neh. 1:6).

- Isaiah: *"Woe is me, for I am ruined!*
        Because I am a man of unclean lips,
        And I live among a people of unclean lips" (Isa. 6:5).

- The tax-gatherer: *" 'God be merciful to me, the sinner!' "*
        (Luke 18:13).

The next step is spiritual mourning. "Blessed are those who mourn, for they shall be comforted" (Matt. 5:4). Every person I know readily acknowledges that he or she sins. Some persons are sincerely sorry for their mistakes and would genuinely like to overcome them. But they stop short of mourning for those sins because they mistakenly believe that on their own they can work such things out. Or, perhaps they feel little or no accountability to God or others for their sins. A person led by the Holy Spirit has no such illusions. That person views himself with a reality which leads directly to spiritual mourning. Believers must experience spiritual poverty and mourning before they can be filled with the Holy Spirit. This mourning is a result of the Holy Spirit's conviction that the sins we committed, the mistakes made, and the circumstances we face are a result of our own choices. We are responsible to God for our spiritual need.

The person who mourns spiritually is one who begins to take account of his life, recognizes his need, and is broken. It is this person that God comforts and guides into the kingdom.

The next stage in entering the kingdom is to experience humility or meekness. "Blessed are the gentle, for they shall inherit the earth" (Matt. 5:5). Meek persons are willing and ready to submit to the Lord. They have exhausted their own efforts and resources. They are impoverished in spirit and mournful due to their spiritual condition. The meek person stops pretending, protecting self, and considering personal interests as primary. Recognition of their true spiritual condition puts an end forever to pride and arrogance. They place their entire lives in the hands of the Lord.

Meek persons are willing to be taught kingdom truths from the King. They are ready to listen and willing to learn.

The most significant changes in our lives occur when we are willing to seriously take stock of our lives. Only the Holy Spirit can provide the ability to view ourselves as we are in respect to others and to God. The meek person recognizes that God alone determines life, its quality, and its meaning. The verse that states those who are meek "shall inherit the earth" affirms the truth that all things are ours because all things are His.

As we move through spiritual poverty, spiritual mourning, and true meekness, we draw near to the righteousness required in the kingdom of God. "Blessed are those who hunger and thirst for righteousness, for they shall be satisfied" (Matt. 5:6). As believers and kingdom citizens we are characterized by the very righteousness of God. But how do we experience this righteousness when our lives are spiritually impoverished? There must be a deep hunger for righteousness. It is impossible to hunger for the kingdom of God and not desire to be righteous. Scripture describes two aspects of righteousness. The first is *legal*—when we are declared to be righteous by faith in Jesus Christ. The second is *moral*—when we, in

As a result of spiritual need and hunger, the believer is ready to be used in the kingdom of God.

fact, become like Him through the power and work of the Holy Spirit. The first aspect is realized the moment we are saved. The second is experienced over a lifetime of living in the kingdom of God.

Rewind. *Fill in the blanks to define two aspects of righteousness.*
_____ *righteousness = declared to be righteous by faith in Jesus Christ*
_____ *righteousness = becoming like Jesus Christ by the power of the Holy Spirit*

Legal righteousness refers to the fact of being declared righteous through faith in Christ. Moral righteousness is becoming like Jesus through the power of the Holy Spirit. It involves a deep desire on the believer's part to live righteously. This desire to be righteous grows out of a continuous, conscious need. It is a desire to be holy and not sinful, to be like Christ and not dominated by the power and desire for sin, and to be victorious in living and not overcome by Satan. The promise Jesus makes is that when the desire for righteousness is present, the fulfillment of that desire surely follows. The Holy Spirit also produces the very life and character of Christ (righteousness) in the believer's life and instills a constant yearning to be like Jesus.

Righteousness is the key to service, and the Beatitudes show us how the believer begins to move from need to service. We become like Christ in order to serve like Him.

Stop and Think! *The first four Beatitudes contain four steps to spiritual satisfaction. Write the four steps to spiritual satisfaction, in the right order, on the four steps below.*

SPIRITUAL SATISFACTION

(The steps are: spiritual poverty, spiritual mourning, experiencing humility, experiencing righteousness.)

We must learn to see others as God sees them and to do whatever is necessary to meet their needs.

The next four Beatitudes are outward expressions of the righteousness that every believer possesses in Christ. Notice how each transforms the believer from receiving to giving. "Blessed are the merciful, for they shall receive mercy" (Matt. 5:7). Believers reflect the mercy of God as they look upon the misery of others and are moved with compassion to help them overcome their suffering. Another dimension of mercy is that we begin to see others (as God saw us) in their spiritual poverty. For believers to see others as God sees them and then to act to meet their needs with mercy, they must have experienced God's grace, mercy and forgiveness.

Following mercy is a pure heart. "Blessed are the pure in heart, for they shall see God" (Matt. 5:8). At first glance, this might be interpreted as an inward quality of purity, but in actuality this verse refers more to a mind which is completely set and focused on Christ and His kingdom. It is a pure heart accompanied by a sincere life. It is the absence of hypocrisy or pretense. The Holy Spirit cleanses our lives as He lives and works within to make us like Christ. "Pure in heart" refers to the outward manifestation of this cleansing.

What exactly is the heart of a kingdom believer? The word *heart* in the Bible often references the personality or whole being of a person. It is the place where "the real you" lives, thinks, and acts—the real you that no one else but God knows or sees. Jesus reigns in the believer's heart, controlling his thoughts, emotions, and will. The heart is Christ's throne in our lives and comes to fullness only when Christ takes control. For that to occur, our hearts must be pure and completely focused on God. Then the outward life is sincere.

The next Beatitude is truly remarkable. "Blessed are the peacemakers, for they shall be called sons of God" (Matt. 5:9). There is great value to one who offers any measure of peace to the world. Persons who counsel a friend to trust God in a difficult marriage, diplomats who bring peace between nations at war, mothers who nurture peace between troubled children, and believers who share the gospel with lost persons are priceless in estimation. A peacemaker is focused on the things of God. He is not ambitious. He is at peace with God, and he is not selfish. He knows the futility of living apart from God, and He knows how to lead others toward God. From his own experience a peacemaker knows what Paul meant when he wrote, "Therefore having been justified by faith, we have peace with God through our Lord Jesus Christ" (Rom. 5:1). Peacemaking is one evidence of belonging to the kingdom.

The final Beatitude is the blessing of persecution. "Blessed are those who have been persecuted for the sake of righteousness, for theirs is the kingdom of heaven" (Matt. 5:10). How can persecution bring blessings and joy? How can pain, rejection, and injury help us in our service to Christ? First, remember that not one of the blessings in the Beatitudes is a result of human wisdom. Rather the blessings are received from God. We cannot be delivered from spiritual poverty or mourning without God's grace. We cannot achieve righteousness on our own. We cannot attain mercy, pure hearts, or make peace without the power of the Holy Spirit working in our lives. This Beatitude does not say that persecution for our Christian stand brings happiness. It says that the blessing comes to the righteous when they *are* persecuted.

When we are righteous, we are like Christ; and like Him, we will be persecuted. Jesus taught that His servants would not be spared the rejection and persecution of the Master (John 15:18-20). Paul reminded Timothy that "all who desire to live godly in Christ Jesus will be persecuted" (2 Tim. 3:12). There is an eternal antagonism between God and everything and everyone who is apart from Him. However, the battle is actually a blessing if we are persecuted for being Christlike.

We are in Christ and the enemies of Christ will come against us as they did Him. We cannot be excused from the conflict of all the ages.

Rewind. *The final four Beatitudes describe the results or expressions of righteousness—mercy, purity, peace, and persecution. Place these on the points of the diagram below.*

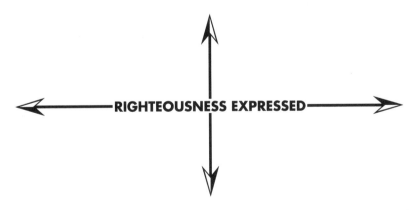

Throughout the remainder of the Sermon on the Mount, the pattern of kingdom living is woven from the strands of reality of the kingdom of God and the righteousness that the kingdom requires. Our lives are patterned after Christ, and the way we live must reflect Him. Believers must model the righteousness of Christ in personal relationships, giving, fasting, prayer, and day-to-day concerns.

Who we are in Christ and how we live affects our ability to accomplish His purposes in the kingdom of God. When we examine the life of Christ and what He taught in the Sermon on the Mount, we discover that service in the kingdom of God is unique and different from what we might expect.

Jesus declared that every believer is, "the salt of the earth … [and] the light of the world" (Matt. 5:13-14). We are to be savor in a tasteless world and light in a dark world. He commands us to shine our light around us so that they "may see your good works, and glorify your Father who is in heaven" (Matt. 5:16). These verses are simple and yet profound in what they teach us about work in the kingdom of God. We are saved from the darkness through Christ and given light to shine back into the darkness. This is the very nature of kingdom work as we join God across the world to build His kingdom. These verses about salt and light reveal the essence of discipleship. They are crucial to our understanding of the Great Commission. They are key to understanding obedience to God and effective and fruitful service to Christ in His kingdom. In short, this is how we take the life of Christ we have been given and put it to the fullest eternal use and significance.

Our relationship to Christ allows us to bring the truth of salvation to the world who needs Him. We have the ability to shine as lights for those lost in the darkness we ourselves have known.

The words *salt* and *light* are metaphors Jesus used to express a single idea in parallel form. Each word brings to mind an obvious example of what it really means to be a Christian. Together, the words indicate that believers are important to God in His kingdom work and to the world for their witness to Christ. These verses reveal important truths for understanding how we can accomplish all that God desires. First, there is a difference between believers and non-believers. We are not like those whose lives have not been redeemed. We are not like those who remain in darkness and are helpless to live life in fullness. We have come from our need for righteousness to salvation in Christ. We have become righteous in Christ and are able to impact our world through His life within us for the glory of God and the building of His kingdom. We lived in decay and under the domination of sin and Satan, but now we are salt in the world, able to bring truth and change to those in bondage. We were lost in the darkness of rebellion against God and unbelief, but now we are light just as Jesus is the Light of the world. Second, we see from this passage that the qualities of salt and light make it impossible for us to find fulfillment apart from being and doing what God has intended. In Christ we are what He Himself is, and it is ludicrous for us not to be salt and not to be light. It is against the very nature of a kingdom believer. John says of Christ: "In Him was life, and the life was the light of men. And the light shines in the darkness, and the darkness did not comprehend it" (John 1:4-5).

These verses do not suggest that we *become* salt and light. Rather they inform us that we *are* salt and light, and our purpose is to accomplish kingdom work in the world.

Jesus clearly expected to do the Father's work, and He expects us to join Him.

Do you have any phobias—fears that really grip you? The only thing that comes close to being a phobia in my life is a feeling I get when I am underground. I do not fear heights, close places, or animals; but being underground where it is dark and damp is a challenge. I went "caving" once in college. While we were in the cave someone decided that we should turn out our lights and experience *total* darkness. It was a scary experience! Then someone lit a small candle. That little candle was a powerful reminder that the smallest light can illuminate the greatest darkness.

Light overcomes darkness just as salt overwhelms the natural taste of anything it touches. The kingdom of God cannot be overcome because Christ cannot be overcome. We have the life of Christ; His light, His salt, and His character live within us. We cannot be overcome by society, sin, or any external foe to the kingdom of God. The only way we can be overcome is if we refuse to be what we have become in Christ. We must not fail the world we have been sent to serve by losing our savor or hiding Christ's light within us.

We have entered the kingdom of God for the purpose of fulfilling the will of God on earth. We have lives to live, the gospel message to share, people to reach, and light to shine! Our world may be under the dark dominion of sin, Satan, and the lusts of the flesh, but we have good news. We offer help and power for those who are lost and helpless. We have Christ within us to share with those in need.

Third, believers have the responsibility to live before the world and minister in such a way that people observe our "good works" and glorify God in heaven. The purpose of our lives in Christ is to share what we have been given—to reveal the glory of God to others. Our service, our success, our accomplishments are only for the purpose of glorifying God before others.

Stop and Think! *Which of the three qualities of salt and light is the most difficult for you—being different from unbelievers, depending on God, or doing good works? What must you change to be salt and light in this area?*

_____

_____

"For by grace you have been saved through faith; and that not of yourselves, it is the gift of God; not as a result of works, that no one should boast. For we are His workmanship, created in Christ Jesus for good works, which God prepared beforehand, that we should walk in them."

Ephesians 2:8-10

How would you describe your life and character in Christ today? Can those around you see Christ manifested daily? Do you live and serve Christ in such a way that people come to Christ and begin to serve Him as you do? It is unfortunate that many believe there is no good thing within us to offer anyone else. When we are redeemed by the grace of God and received into the kingdom of God, we are awarded unique identity as disciples with vital importance to accomplish God's purposes in this world. We are the instruments of God, and we join Him in His kingdom activity. We have, as Paul said, "treasure in earthen vessels, that the surpassing greatness of the power may be of God and not from ourselves" (2 Cor. 4:7). Alone we have no answers, but Christ in us gives us His light and power to accomplish His tasks.

Let's look specifically at how to serve the Lord and do kingdom work. Jesus said, "We must work the works of Him who sent Me, as long as it is day; night is coming, when no man can work" (John 9:4).

Jesus often spoke of His work and our work. Each time He referenced the work, He emphasized that it belonged to the Father. We do not work for God while He sits in heaven watching or perhaps aids our efforts. The Father is the One working out His plan in the world. We are His instruments and servants in fulfilling this plan. The following two verses remind us of exactly how we are to serve the Lord of the harvest.

"But He answered them, 'My Father is working until now, and I Myself am working'" (John 5:17).

"The harvest is plentiful, but the laborers are few; therefore beseech the Lord of the harvest to send out laborers into His harvest" (Luke 10:2).

This great Old Testament passage illustrates the way God does His work through His people.

> *And the Lord said, "I have surely seen the affliction of My people who are in Egypt, and have given heed to their cry because of their taskmasters, for I am aware of their sufferings. So I have come down to deliver them from the power of the Egyptians. … Therefore, come now, and I will send you to Pharaoh, so that you may bring My people … out of Egypt" (Ex. 3:7-8,10).*

Did you notice that God told Moses He was about to deliver His children out of Pharaoh's hand? They were leaving Egypt by the hand and power of God. Did you also notice that God told Moses that he would be His instrument to lead the Israelites? God was doing His work through His servant Moses.

We do not work *for* God, but God works *through* us. It is God who moves in time and history to accomplish His purposes, and we are empowered as His servants to accomplish what He desires. Throughout the Bible, God's people have been called and equipped for special service to Him. Moses led the nation of Israel in God's power. Joshua led them to a land God provided. The judges ruled in God's power. The kings ruled according to God's will to accomplish what He desired. The prophets and biblical writers were filled with the Holy Spirit to declare God's Word.

Years ago I read a book by the famous preacher F.B. Myer who told of a conversation he once had with Hudson Taylor, the most famous missionary to ever take the gospel to China. He said the Lord once told him: "Hudson, I am going to take the gospel to inland China and if you want to walk beside me I will use you to do it."

That is a powerful example of work in the kingdom of God. The work is God's and He alone accomplishes it for His own glory and purposes. God saved us by His grace, He gave us faith to trust Him, and He prepared works for us to accomplish even before the foundation of the world. What a plan! What a relief for every believer who longs to work for the Lord and to accomplish His kingdom purposes! We do not have to invent the kingdom of God or its works. We are not bound by God to create institutions, programs, and dreams to finish His work. He already has planned these things. He is at work and He calls us to join Him.

"Trust in the Lord with all your heart,
And do not lean on your own understanding.
In all your ways acknowledge Him,
And He will make your paths straight.
Do not be wise in your own eyes;
Fear the Lord and turn away from evil."

Proverbs 3:5-7

Working in the Kingdom of God

How do we do this work in the kingdom of God? To find the answer to this important question, we must refer to Jesus' life and ministry. He is our example and our leader. He reveals the Father to us, and we follow Him to accomplish the Father's will.

Do you remember how the Father described Jesus when He was on earth? At Jesus' baptism the Father said, "This is My beloved Son, in whom I am well-pleased" (Matt. 3:17). At the transfiguration He said, "This is My beloved Son, with whom I am well-pleased; listen to Him!" (Matt. 17:5). Jesus did everything the Father asked Him to do and accomplished everything God wanted Him to accomplish. Our identification with Christ begins with salvation, but it moves us to kingdom work. Jesus said, "Truly, truly, I say to you, he who believes in Me, the works that I do shall he do also; and greater works than these shall he do; because I go to the Father" (John 14:12).

Never do anything or go anywhere in ministry unless the Father sends you. If you do, even with the best of intentions and motives, you will be working against Him and the growth of His kingdom.

Think for a moment about what this verse really means. We who believe in Christ will do the very works that Jesus Christ did when He was on earth! This is one of the most amazing verses in the entire Bible. How can we do what Jesus Christ did? We certainly cannot interpret this verse to mean that we possess the natural capacity to do anything for God. As a matter of fact, if we think that we can do anything in our own strength and in our own understanding, we violate the clear teaching of Scripture.

Jesus began His ministry by announcing that the kingdom of God had come. He then proved it by teaching and preaching with life-changing authority. He performed many miracles, healed the sick, raised the dead, and drove demons out of people's lives. He accomplished the works of the Father and presented them as complete on the cross when He declared, "It is finished!"

But how can we do what Jesus did? Can we in our own strength raise the dead, drive demons from people, walk on water, calm the sea, stop the wind, come back from the dead? No, of course not. But we can do anything He has done if we have His power and presence within our lives. Jesus Himself explains in John 14:12 and John 15:1-17. He said that He chose us and ordained us to bear lasting fruit (v. 16). To do that, we must abide in Him (John 15:4), abide in His Word (John 15:7), and abide in His love (John 15:9). Without Christ we can do nothing (John 15:5), but with Him all things are possible.

If we look closely at the life and ministry of Christ, we learn that He brought the kingdom of God to earth by working the works of the

Father in four specific ways. If we truly follow Christ in all things, we will consider these four truths as we serve Him. Each bears examination and commitment.

• *Jesus went only where He was sent by the Father.* Time and time again we find in the Gospels that Jesus never did anything for the Father unless He was sent to accomplish a particular task. He certainly could have accomplished good anywhere He went, but Christ never chose to go anywhere. He submitted to the will of the Father, and He went only where He was sent. In fact, the Gospel of John records 27 times where Jesus did something, went somewhere, or taught something simply because the Father sent Him. John the Baptist said of Christ, "He whom God has sent speaks the words of God; for He gives the Spirit without measure" (John 3:34). Jesus said, "I have come down from heaven, not to do My own will, but the will of Him who sent Me" (John 6:38).

Jesus inaugurated the kingdom of God, and we are commissioned to continue what He began in His strength and presence.

If Jesus submitted to doing only what God wanted and going only where He was sent, how can we do less? We cannot tell God where we will do kingdom work and where we will live and serve Him. We cannot presume to know where to go and what to do. Jesus was sent to earth first and then to various places during His ministry. We are also a "sent" people. Jesus said, "Peace be with you; as the Father has sent Me, I also send you" (John 20:21). The Greek words for *sent* and *send* are different. The first means *to be sent with the authority of a ruler or Lord*. We get our word *apostle* from this word. The other means *to be commissioned, to accomplish the works of God in the same manner as Christ did*. We then are extensions of Christ's work in the world.

Kingdom work must never be confused with activity, and fulfilling God's purposes cannot always be measured by our evaluation of success.

Stop and Think! *Read John 14:12. How are you doing the same works Jesus did? How are you doing greater works than He did?*

_____

_____

_____

• *Jesus did only what He saw the Father doing.* It is amazing to realize that Christ, who is fully God and fully man, submitted His will to the Father and did only what the Father showed Him to do.

"Truly, truly, I say to you, the Son can do nothing of Himself, unless it is something He sees the Father doing; for whatever the Father does, these things the Son also does in like manner. For the Father loves the Son, and shows Him all things that He Himself is doing; and greater works than these will He show Him, that you may marvel" (John 5:19-20).

We can only know the Father's works through our relationship with Jesus Christ. For many years I believed I needed to work for the Lord and then present Him with the fruit of my labors. If I got into trouble or experienced a season of frustration or failure, then I asked for His strength and guidance. I thought God's work depended upon me. But Jesus Christ Himself claimed only to do what He saw the Father doing in the world. Jesus always knew the right thing to do at the right time. How can we ever expect to do anything for God when He asks only that we join Him in a relationship that He might work through us?

• *Jesus never initiated anything on His own.* Several times in the Gospel of John Jesus emphasized that His actions were only at the initiative of the Father. For example, He said:

"I can do nothing on My own initiative" (John 5:30).

"I did not speak on My own initiative, but the Father Himself who sent Me has given Me commandment, what to say, and what to speak" (John 12:49).

"The words that I say to you I do not speak on My own initiative, but the Father abiding in Me does His works" (John 14:10).

We are to be like Christ in all respects, and nothing could be more important than to hear from Him before we speak or teach.

These verses affirm that we should refrain from initiating anything on our own. Kingdom work is the Father's responsibility, and He alone will give us guidance and direction. This does not imply that we should sit around and wait until we receive a special revelation from God to work in His kingdom. We have daily tasks to accomplish in obedience to His will. We are to pray, work, teach, evangelize, and live under the authority of His Word. We are to exercise these disciplines until He leads us to a specific task. God promised to reveal

Himself to us, and He reveals Himself through prayer, Bible study, the Holy Spirit, circumstances, and fellow believers.

God desires from us an attitude of expectancy and obedience. We dare not replace the best of kingdom things with merely good things. I once read about a man who founded a great Christian organization. Someone asked him how he came up with the idea and he replied, "God purposed it and I thought it." This statement is pivotal. Out of our personal relationship and daily walk with Christ, He speaks to us concerning the Father's will. We learn from Christ *what to do*. We also learn *how to do* God's work, God's way, and for God's glory.

If we seek the Lord with all our heart, mind, soul, and strength, we will receive from Him the direction we need. God does not usually give us all the answers to our questions when we ask them. He gives us the understanding we need as we need it and when it best suits His plans and purposes.

* *Jesus only spoke what He heard the Father speaking.* The verses above indicate that Jesus waited on the Father to reveal to Him what He needed to accomplish. Once again Jesus stated that He could do nothing on His own initiative but, "I speak these things as the Father taught Me" (John 8:28). He did not rebuke, encourage, preach, teach, or speak at all until He first heard from the Father.

Do you speak to the Father before you teach, preach, or speak to the people? Do you spend time with Him before making major decisions in your life which affect yourself, your family, your business? Jesus again emphasized this when He stated, "When He, the Spirit of truth, comes, He will guide you into all the truth; for He will not speak on His own initiative, but whatever He hears, He will speak; and He will disclose to you what is to come" (John 16:13).

Do not plan for God and run ahead of His will for your life or the ministry of your church. Seek Him and you will find everything you need.

Stop and Think! *Match the following Scripture passages with the sentence which best summarizes each passage.*

John 6:38   *Jesus only spoke what He heard the Father speaking.*

John 5:19-20   *Jesus only went where He was sent by the Father.*

John 5:30   *Jesus never initiated anything on His own.*

John 7:27   *Jesus did only what He saw the Father doing.*

If the Holy Spirit of God and Jesus Christ who is God will not speak until they hear from the Father, we can do no less if we want to be effective in our ministry in the kingdom of God.

Carefully examine your life in Christ. Your identity in Christ makes you unique. Are you living under that identity in such a way that all those around you know you are a Christian, totally devoted to following Christ and living according to His Word? Is your service in the kingdom of God modeled after Jesus' example? Do you find yourself doing the works that Christ did as He stated in John 14:12?

God created us to accomplish His works. If we are living or serving beneath the standard of His will for our lives, we will never experience complete joy and fulfillment no matter what we try or how hard we work.

chapter 5

THE CHURCH AND THE KINGDOM OF GOD

chapter 5

THE CHURCH AND THE KINGDOM OF GOD

> *"I also say to you that you are Peter, and upon this rock I will build My church; and the gates of Hades shall not overpower it. I will give you the keys of the kingdom of heaven; and whatever you shall bind on earth shall be bound in heaven, and whatever you shall loose on earth shall be loosed in heaven."*
>
> *Matthew 16:18-19*

Have you ever noticed the unusual names of some churches? Some I enjoy remembering are: *Hanging Dog Baptist Church, Burnout Baptist Church, Little Hope Baptist Church, Mt. Nebo No. 2,* and *Holy Church of Love and Unity No. 3.* I can only imagine how such names came to be. But every church is like every child—beautiful to the Lord like a child is beautiful to a parent. Every church is special to the King, and each one has a special place in God's kingdom purposes.

The relationship between the church and the kingdom of God is essential in our lives and our service to the Lord. In fact, without a proper understanding of this relationship we cannot fully understand either the kingdom or the church. The kingdom brings the church into perspective, and the church points to the kingdom. In this chapter we will make a brief examination of the nature and mission of the church. For further study and help consider *The Church: God's People on Mission* by Laney L. Johnson and *The Baptist Faith and Message* by Herschel H. Hobbs (Convention Press).

The kingdom of God is the reign of God in the lives of believers as manifested by His activity in, through, and around their lives. The kingdom of God is the key reality of history and is growing toward fulfillment each day. Nothing can stop the kingdom of God from advancing because nothing can stop God and Jesus Christ His Son. The kingdom was inaugurated by Christ at the beginning of His public ministry and will be consummated when He returns to earth.

The church can be defined in simple terms as *a gathered assembly of believers*. This definition is derived from Scripture. The word used most often for church is *ecclesia*. As used by the biblical writers, *ecclesia* means *a gathering of God's people*. Our word *church* comes from the older English word *kirk*. This word has the same meaning as ecclesia. The word *synagogue* also has a similar meaning to *ecclesia*. These words all point to a gathering or assembling of God's people to worship Him and study His Word.

94

Throughout Scripture we see the church as local and global. Sometimes the term *church* refers to the global or universal church. Universal does not mean that all persons are in the church, but rather it refers to the church throughout the ages. The church as we know it began at Pentecost and has since continued to grow and develop. The global church is the collective body of Christ, made up of believers around the world and throughout history. This is the church Christ promised in Matthew 16:18 and Paul referred to in Ephesians: "He put all things in subjection under His feet, and gave Him as head over all things to the church" (1:22), and, "There is one body" (4:4).

In the New Testament, most references to the church refer to a local congregation in a specific geographic location, for instance: "Paul, ... to the church of God which is at Corinth" (1 Cor. 1:1-2). Sometimes a writer referred to several local congregations in a geographical region, for example, "Paul, ... to the churches of Galatia" (Gal. 1:1-2). One letter is obviously addressed to a specific church and one to a number of churches in the region of Galatia. Most New Testament teachings address particular concerns within local congregations. Even so, the teachings apply to all believers.

The church began as the fulfillment of a promise from Jesus Christ on the day of Pentecost as recorded in Acts, chapter 2. On this day the Holy Spirit came from heaven to earth and entered the lives of the small band of believers who had assembled at the command of Christ in the upper room to pray and wait for the Spirit's coming.

"When the day of Pentecost had come, they were all together in one place. And suddenly there came from heaven a noise like a violent, rushing wind, and it filled the whole house where they were sitting. ... And they were all filled with the Holy Spirit and began to speak with other tongues, as the Spirit was giving them utterance" (Acts 2:1-2,4).

What a day and what an event to establish the church! Three thousand persons were added to the original band of 120, and history changed forever. Since that day the church has been functioning as the chief agent of the kingdom.

In addition to the church as a local body of believers who gather to worship and serve the Lord and the church as the global body of Christ, some have described the church as the invisible body of Christ. What most mean by the term *invisible* is that the true church is made up of redeemed persons while local churches often have unsaved members. However, the church can never really be invisible because

The Father founded the kingdom, Jesus Christ is its focus, and the Holy Spirit is the facilitator. The church is not a new creation, distinct and separate from the kingdom of God, but rather a developing entity designed to fulfill God's kingdom agenda.

The church is local and global. It is made up of the redeemed saints of God in all places, at all times.

believers are salt and light of the world (Matt. 5:13-16). In Christ, it is God's purpose to save us from "every lawless deed and purify for Himself a people for His own possession, zealous for good deeds" (Titus 2:14). We are created for good works to show the world our Savior and Lord. The church is always a real presence in the world.

Rewind. *Match the phrase on the left with the phrase on the right which best completes the sentence.*

> • *the same as the kingdom of God.*

The church is   • *a developing entity designed to fulfill God's agenda for the kingdom.*

> • *not really related to the kingdom of God.*

The church is certainly related to the kingdom of God, but it is not the same as the kingdom. The truth is found in the second statement in the activity above. God has designed the church to fulfill His kingdom agenda.

The Nature of the Church

What is the nature of the church and how does this relate to the Father's kingdom agenda? The church must be described in the light of the nature of Christ and in some sense the kingdom of God. In his famous work, *All the Doctrines of the Bible*, Herbert Lockyer lists 29 different names for the church which describe its nature. They are:

The Holy Spirit assembles the church for worship, fellowship, and discipleship while He sends the church out in evangelism and ministry.

1. The Body of Christ—
   Ephesians 1:22-23; Colossians 1:24.
2. The Bride of Christ—
   Ephesians 5:31-33; 2 Corinthians 11:2-3;
   Revelation 19:7; 21:9.
3. The Glory of Christ—
   Ephesians 3:21; 2 Corinthians 8:23.
4. The House of Christ—
   Hebrews 3:6.
5. The House of God—
   1 Timothy 3:15; Hebrews 10:21.
6. The Habitation of God—

Ephesians 2:19-22; 1 Peter 2:4-5.

7. The Temple of God—
    1 Corinthians 3:16-17.
8. The Temple of the Living God—
    2 Corinthians 6:16.
9. God's Building—
    1 Corinthians 3:9.
10. God's Husbandry—
    1 Corinthians 3:9.
11. God's Heritage—
    1 Peter 5:3.
12. The Church of God—
    Acts 20:28.
13. The Church of the Living God—
    1 Timothy 3:15.
14. The Church of the First Born—
    Hebrews 12:23.
15. The Israel of God—
    Galatians 6:16.
16. The Flock of God—
    1 Peter 5:2.
17. The City of the Living God—
    Hebrews 12:22.
18. Mount Zion—
    Hebrews 12:22.
19. New Jerusalem—
    Revelation 21:2.
20. Heavenly Jerusalem—
    Galatians 4:26; Hebrews 12:22.
21. Spiritual House—
    1 Peter 2:5.
22. The Pillar and Ground of Truth—
    1 Timothy 3:15.
23. The Family in Heaven and Earth—
    Ephesians 3:15.
24. A Mystery—
    Ephesians 3:9; 5:32; Colossians 1:25-26.
25. The Light of the World—
    Matthew 5:14.
26. The Golden Candlesticks—

The many names by which the church is called in Scripture all point to the ownership and nature of the church.

Revelation 1:20.
27. The Salt of the Earth—
     Matthew 5:13.
28. One Bread—
     1 Corinthians 10:17.
29. An Elect Race ... Royal Priesthood ... Holy Nation—
     1 Peter 2:9.[1]

Rewind. *Review the list of 29 references to the church. Mark those that refer to the church's ownership with a "O" and those that refer to the church's nature with an "N."*

It is amazing to see the number of references to the church found in the New Testament that do not even use the word *church*. Most of these references refer to the ownership and nature of the church. References 1-17 in the list above refer in various ways to the ownership of the church. References 18-29 give insight into the nature of the church. The most common references describe the church as a body of believers, the body of Christ, the bride of Christ, and a building of persons in Christ.

The church is a supernatural work of God in Christ, empowered by the Holy Spirit to accomplish God's work.

The church, then, like the kingdom of God, is made up of regenerate persons who focus their worship and service on Christ. The church is gathered and sent simultaneously to fulfill the Great Commission (Matt. 28:19-20).

Stop and Think! *According to Matthew 29:18-20, who shares the co-mission of the church?*

_____

_____

_____

The church is able to accomplish the work of Jesus Christ because the Holy Spirit equips it for service through spiritual gifts. The Holy Spirit is present within the life of every Christian to build Christlike character, to comfort, guide, teach, and seal the believer in Christ forever, and to bestow spiritual gifts for service to God in His church.

It is important to remember that although the Holy Spirit works in our lives to do works of service to the Lord, it is Christ Himself who is the Head of the church. The church is His body, His bride, and His building used to reflect His glory and to accomplish His kingdom purposes. Christ bestows the Holy Spirit, who in turn gifts believers for this work. The signature New Testament passage which speaks of Christ's rule over the church is Ephesians 4:11-16.

> *"He gave some as apostles, and some as prophets, and some as evangelists, and some as pastors and teachers, for the equipping of the saints for the work of service, to the building up of the body of Christ; until we all attain to the unity of the faith, and of the knowledge of the Son of God, to a mature man, to the measure of the stature which belongs to the fulness of Christ. As a result, we are no longer to be children, tossed here and there by waves, and carried about by every wind of doctrine, by the trickery of men, by craftiness in deceitful scheming; but speaking the truth in love, we are to grow up in all aspects into Him, who is the head, even Christ, from whom the whole body, being fitted and held together by that which every joint supplies, according to the proper working of each individual part, causes the growth of the body for the building up of itself in love" (Eph. 4:11-16).*

The church is the body of Christ. He is the Head of the church, and it exists to do His work in the world.

This passage is the essence of the life of a church which gathers to worship and departs to serve Christ. Any congregation of believers who purposes to fulfill the truth of this passage is totally in tune with God's kingdom agenda.

A. H. Strong wrote a classic definition of the church in his famous *Systematic Theology.*

> "The individual church may be defined as that smaller company of regenerate persons, who, in any given community, unite themselves voluntarily together, in accordance with Christ's laws, for the purpose of securing the complete establishment of his kingdom in themselves and in the world."[2]

Stop and Think. *Review A. H. Strong's definition of the church. Circle the words you consider the most significant for an accurate definition of the church. Then write your personal definition for a church.*

_____

_____

_____

_____

As believers and church members in service to Jesus, we must focus on the same things as Jesus. We must be working to establish the kingdom of God wherever we go and whatever we do.

The Mission of the Church

Scripture not only points us to the nature of the church, but it also points to its mission. The mission of the church must be in keeping with the kingdom of God and God's agenda to fulfill His redemptive purposes in the world.

The Great Commission defines God's mission (which is our mission) in the world. The Commission is the Lord's marching orders for every believer and the church. Understanding the meaning and full implication of the Commission is crucial if we are to accomplish the work of the church God's way and if we are to carry out His kingdom agenda. This is the age of the church. As the church sows the seed of the gospel, it reaps a harvest of people who respond to the message of Christ. This is the age of evangelism and discipleship as more and more believers enter the kingdom of God and become part of the fellowship of the church.

God has been on mission to redeem lost humanity since Adam and Eve's sin in the garden of Eden. It is our privilege to acknowledge His kingdom plan and to join Him in the ministry to which He calls us.

While the church is *not* the kingdom, it *is* the agent and servant of the kingdom, and serves as its hands and feet for accomplishing the Father's kingdom agenda. As the instrument God has chosen to bring His message of redemption in Christ to the world, the church must focus on the work God Himself is doing. In this sense kingdom growth and church growth go hand in hand. Church growth occurs as

God works through His people to accomplish His purposes. As this transpires, kingdom growth happens.

Kingdom growth is a result of believers and churches applying kingdom principles and truths to their lives. A church must see itself strategically positioned between the truth of God and lost persons. With reconciliation to God as its purpose of ministry, the church must bring the gospel of the kingdom to persons and lead them to a saving faith and knowledge of God through Christ. In this sense the church is a kingdom agent which stands between two worlds—the world lost and without God and the world of God's kingdom. The church must forever stand in the gap between a gracious God and a lost humanity offering the gospel and the ministry of reconciliation.

Rewind. *Mark the following statements T (true) or F (false).*

___ *The mission of the church is not related to the kingdom of God.*
___ *The growth of the church and the kingdom of God are related.*
___ *The church is a kingdom agent, the bridge between a gracious God and lost humanity.*

The nature of the kingdom of God prevents us from being sheltered in our private worlds of selfish pursuits and concerns. We are not only part of the church of the living Lord Jesus Christ, but also a part of His kingdom.

The first statement in the activity above is false. The last two statements are true. The last statement is especially important. The church is God's kingdom agent in the world. The relationship between the church and the kingdom of God is also important in regard to unity among believers. Often during 20th-century Christian history, there have been calls for and attempts to bring unification to believers and denominations. For the most part, these efforts have been futile and probably will continue to be futile. Why? Because it's the wrong focus. The kingdom of God contains, but is not subject to, various denominations, theologies, and parachurch movements. It encompasses all of them, even when these are in conflict.

The existence of one monolithic, organized institutional church to which every Christian belongs is neither necessary nor desirable. The Lord has one church, the body of Christ to which every believer belongs by way of God's grace in Christ. The variety in kinds of churches and denominations reflects the freedom and diversity of the body of Christ as it fulfills God's kingdom agenda. The goal is not a unified church to which all belong but the expansion of the kingdom of God to its fullest in every sphere of life on earth.

Stop and Think! *Write your personal reaction to the statement: "The goal (of kingdom people) is not a unified church to which all belong but the expansion of the kingdom of God to its fullest in every sphere of life on earth."*

The kingdom is truly invisible and mysterious. It cannot be seen, understood, or appreciated by lost persons. A person must be brought to spiritual life by the Holy Spirit and saved by God's grace through faith in Christ to even comprehend it. It comes by revelation through a personal relationship with Christ by which all truth is ultimately known.

_____

_____

_____

_____

Believers and churches join God on mission by following biblical kingdom principles. We must evangelize lost persons wherever we encounter them. We must disciple believers throughout their lives with the goal of presenting them complete in Christ when He returns. We must develop and encourage fellowship among believers which matches that found in the New Testament. This means teaching people how to cultivate commitment and interest in one another that glorifies Christ and builds His body, the church. We must minister to those in need as Jesus taught and commanded. We must worship God in ways that bring glory to Him. These kingdom functions are the constant responsibilities of every believer and every church.

The kingdom of God is driving history and includes all that God has done and is presently doing on earth. We cannot always see or understand how He tears down strongholds of evil and sin, how He uses rulers and nations, or how He will save multitudes of blasphemers, but we know He will. The real question is not how or when He chooses to work but *why*. He works in His world because He has purposed to do so. He has chosen to redeem His elect to the ends of the earth among persons of every tribe and tongue in the world.

The task of the church is to look at earthly persons through kingdom eyes and see them as God sees them. We must be compelled to share the gospel so that they might come to know their Creator and Redeemer in Christ.

Events already have been set in motion by the coming of Christ and the calling out of the church that will fulfill God's kingdom purpose.

- The Father will act in His sovereignty to establish His kingdom.
- Believers in the church will preach the gospel around the world.
- Persons will receive the gospel, be saved, and follow Christ.
- The church will be prepared and purified (discipled) to accomplish His purposes in the world.
- Evil and Satan will be completely destroyed.

Our world is moving in the direction God intends. Suffering, natural disasters, apostasy, the rise of evil, the fall of church leaders, and other things cannot stop what God has set in motion. These events are only signs that the kingdom of God is moving into position to receive its returning King. The kingdom of God causes the church to move into the world with a commission and a compassion. Christ commands that we go, and He goes with us. At the same time, we join Christ against evil with His power to destroy its influence wherever it is found.

The Uniqueness of the Kingdom and the Church

The relationship between the kingdom of God and the church is unique and very important. What are the basic differences between the kingdom of God and the church? In most theological discussions, scholars come to one of the three following conclusions.

- Some believe Jesus never intended to establish the church because He mentioned it only twice in the Gospels. Those who hold this position believe the two references in Matthew are not in the original texts and that the church was a later development instituted by the disciples when the kingdom did not come as they hoped. It is not the purpose of this study to give attention to this theory, but we can say that two references in the Gospels are adequate. The fact that seven churches are addressed by the living Christ and mentioned in Revelation 1–3 discounts such a theory.

Jesus Christ has determined to build His church by giving believers the message that has the power to change the lives of persons.

- Others believe that the kingdom of God and the church are in essence the same thing. Those who hold this position believe that Jesus combined them in such a way that that the church is the comprehensive work of God on earth and the kingdom comes in fullness at the end of time. This view imposes an interpretation on Scripture, especially the Gospels, that must justify Jesus' use of the term *kingdom* or conclude that He misinterpreted history as it would unfold. Jesus is the true and living Word of God. He was not mistaken about the kingdom.

The church is the truest visible expression of the kingdom of God on earth.

• The view which best fits Scripture and the development of history is that the kingdom of God and the church are separate but related entities. The kingdom of God has to do with the reign of God, while the church relates to the gathered and ministering assembly of believers. The kingdom creates the church, and the church witnesses to the kingdom. The church is the instrument of the kingdom to fulfill the purposes of God on earth. The kingdom is eternal while the church is temporal in the sense that the church is of this age and time. The church was sent into the world as a missionary force to bear witness to Christ. The kingdom of God was already present on earth. A person must be born again from the Holy Spirit to enter both the kingdom and the church. In local congregations persons who are not saved may join a congregation, but they are not part of the church, as God intended it to be. Much of the reality of the kingdom is ideal in the sense that it is perfect. The church on earth is not always ideal and can only approximate the perfection of Christ's rule when He comes. Each believer and church has a kingdom stewardship responsibility. This creates a sense of urgency and importance which we will now examine.

Rewind. *Fill in the blanks below to summarize the relationship of the kingdom of God and the church.*

1. The kingdom of God focuses on the _____ of God and the church the _____ of believers.

2. The kingdom of God _____ the church and the church _____ to the kingdom.

3. The church is the visible _____ of the kingdom of God while the kingdom is _____ in the sense that it is perfect.

In review, the kingdom focuses on the reign of God, while the focus of the church is on the gathered and ministering assembly of God's people. The kingdom of God creates the church, and the church bears witness to the kingdom. The church is the visible expression of the kingdom, while the kingdom is ideal and perfect.

The Urgency of the Kingdom of God
The church has a message and ministry of reconciliation which has

great power to deliver those in the bondage of sin, the domination of the devil, and the power of the flesh and the mind (Eph. 2:1-3). This combination is a stewardship which cannot be taken lightly nor easily disregarded without great spiritual peril. Suppose you were a lifeguard and observed someone drowning but refused to help? Ignoring the victim would be a violation of your calling as a lifesaver and a disregard of your abilities and training. It is unthinkable that any lifeguard would willingly let someone die. Can we feel any differently toward lost persons and sinful persons? We have been given the gift of life by Christ, and we can give the gift of life to others by sharing the gospel with them and ministering to them in ways which point them to a saving relationship and fellowship with Christ. We are under the authority of Christ and can rescue such persons from their sin and separation from God. We are "ambassadors for Christ, as though God were entreating through us" (2 Cor. 5:20). This relationship to Christ ignites an urgency to make us bold in our work for the Lord.

We are members of the Messianic community which reveals the nature of the kingdom and hastens its coming. Effective churches and healthy congregations all have a kingdom focus which they never lose or change.

In addition, because the church tangibly represents spiritual reality of the kingdom of God on earth, the life of the church must be marked by holiness and righteousness. We cannot say to those outside, "Come as you are and stay the way you are." Believers must demonstrate a devotion to Christ which indicates we are complete in Him. The true kingdom saint is a person who *becomes* something in order to *do* something. We must become like Christ, live like Christ, and think like Christ in order to do the works of Christ.

We cannot be merely consumers of ministry and spiritual babies taking only what is offered in the church. We cannot place unreasonable demands upon church leaders, pastors, and fellow believers which deplete their spiritual energy and resources. As believers, we benefit from belonging to the body of Christ and are enriched as we gather with fellow Christians for edification, worship and service. We are not, however, saved only to be served by others until our personal needs are met. First, we commit ourselves to the Lord, next to other believers, and then to those outside of Christ. God does not intend that we belong to a "virtual" congregation, isolated in our private worlds, and venturing out only on Sundays for spiritual refreshment and nourishment. To function as God planned, we cannot participate only in television congregations and radio audiences. We must learn to love the unlovely, forbear those who annoy us, and fellowship with those who are different from us. We

As a part of the body of Christ, we must be willing to say, "There is nothing I will not do, nothing I will not give, nowhere I will not go to serve Christ."

must take what we receive from the Lord, go into all the world and give it away. As a kingdom community on mission with God, serving Him and accomplishing His tasks, we will see our churches grow not only in numbers, but also in spiritual depth, ministry, and missions. The church is God's agent for His cosmic purpose. In this sense, each and every local church is a symbol of God's kingdom which has come to earth in Christ.

We were *created* by God as unique and special persons. We are *called* by Him to enter a personal relationship. We are *converted* from our sin and darkness to light and fellowship with God through His grace to us in Christ. We have *surrendered* our lives to Him and *committed* ourselves to His purposes. We have been *incorporated* into His body, and we have *received* a world-changing commission from Him to go into all the world and to make disciples of all people. We *work with Him* to fulfill His purposes as the kingdom advances, and with fellow believers we *await* its consummation at the return of Christ.

Rewind. *Circle the italicized words in the previous paragraph as a review and summary of your responsibilities as a kingdom citizen and church member.*

Until the triumphant return of our Lord, we live in the time of the church. The Lord has returned to heaven, the Holy Spirit has come to live in our lives, and the Father has entrusted us to complete the work He began in Christ. As we face the challenges of today, our task is great. The kingdom and the church are mysteries which only God Himself understands. But the mystery began to unfold in Christ and will be completely revealed when He returns.

---

[1]Dr. Herbert Lockyer, *All the Doctrines of the Bible* (Grand Rapids: Zondervan Publishing House, 1964), 231-232.
[2]Augustus H. Strong, *Systematic Theology* Vol. III (Philadelphia: American Baptist Publication Society, 1909), 890.

chapter 6

FOR THINE IS THE KINGDOM

chapter 6

FOR THINE IS THE KINGDOM

God is on mission and we are commanded to join Him in His task. The Great Commission gives churches a character and a way of life which is truly unique from other religions or humanitarian institutions. The church is the kingdom of God organized for its work. As believers gather around the earth, they are the visible manifestation of the kingdom of God. Each church is a messianic community functioning as a mission center for God's purposes. We must align our thinking and our work with this mission.

"This gospel of the kingdom shall be preached in the whole world for a witness to all the nations, and then the end shall come."

Matthew 24:14

The Great Commission is Christ's mandate until He returns from heaven. It makes missions the focus of our activities as it sends us out into the world to gather those the Father is saving and redeeming. Then it instructs us to baptize them and to teach them to observe all that Christ commands. It is this command that must direct the kingdom strategy of both individuals and churches untill Jesus returns.

The Kingdom of God and the Church

The church, both local and global, is the agency on earth for doing the work of the kingdom. A local church must constitute and organize itself around some charter of purpose and work. A church is a church because it focuses on fulfilling the will and the work of God in establishing His kingdom throughout the earth.

Stop and Think! *Based on observing its schedule, budget, programs, and leaders, what is the purpose of your church?*

_____

_____

_____

The work of the church, then, is missions. Every local church should evaluate its teaching, ministry, fellowship, evangelism, and worship to determine if its focus is the entire world. Churches that focus only on the needs and desires of the congregation are not in harmony with God's commands. Likewise, churches which limit their outreach to local areas and only target numerical growth hinder the Holy Spirit's ministry and prevent their members from growing into fully committed disciples. It is also possible for a church to be so focused on international missions that local evangelism and ministry are ignored. We cannot limit the gospel which is for all people by our lack of faith or vision. As believers we are not limited, and we are not restricted to any one method, culture, or nation. We can have an enormous impact preaching the gospel around the world.

The only way for a believer or a church to fully understand the kingdom of God in this age is to rise above the restraints of limited thinking and view the world from a global perspective. Jesus Christ was born incarnate for every person who has ever lived or ever would live on earth. His teachings are transcultural and apply to people of every generation. He died on the cross for all people, and He lives today so that, through Him, all might live.

We cannot fully surrender to Him or His purposes until we view the churches as mission centers. Local churches cannot adequately develop and function as Christ intends without organizing all programs, ministries, and activities to fulfill the Great Commission. Too often churches are preoccupied with themselves, their members, and their own interests while mission opportunities beg for leftover time, resources, and leadership. A church must first define itself with an outward view, then an inward view. Our temptation is to define our Christian lives and church experiences from an inward view. Churches without priorities can major on church growth efforts, teaching doctrines, building buildings, starting support groups, and protecting members from cultural evils while they ignore their primary task—taking the gospel to the world.

Stop and Think! *How would you change your church's schedule, budget, programs, and leaders to reflect the true purpose of the church?*

_____

_____

Jesus Christ gave us a Commission that includes the world. That commission includes a local, regional and world-wide responsibility.

"The Son of Man did not come to be served, but to serve, and to give His life a ransom for many."

Mark 10:45

The Great Commission commands us to witness to those outside the kingdom of God. Jesus gave the disciples a picture of the gospel spreading in concentric circles beginning at Jerusalem and invading the world. We must not wait until all our personal needs are satisfied before we sacrificially give and go to our world. We need to be obedient to Christ and align ourselves and our churches with His will. Churches are enlistment centers for missions. It is our responsibility to reach persons with the gospel, bring them into our fellowships, and then train them to go forth with the gospel. Churches are missions education centers and the Bible is the central text in preparing the hearts and lives of God's people to "Go ... and make disciples of all nations" (Matt. 28:19). Churches are sending agencies, commanded to release their members under the direction of the Holy Spirit to share the good news not only where they are, but also with the entire world. Often, however, we act in the spirit of a bumper sticker I saw recently which read, "Think globally, act locally!" We think about persons on other continents we do not know who need Christ, but we restrict our efforts and concerns to those around us.

Our churches are not safe havens from the challenges of spiritual hardships and warfare. We cannot be removed from our cultures no matter how decadent they might be.

Rewind. *List three ways the church facilitates missions.*

_____

_____

_____

What are your thoughts on the statement, "Think globally, act locally!"

_____

_____

As we have already seen, the church facilitates missions by serving as enlistment centers, education and training centers, and sending agencies. We must disciple and train believers to be fully devoted, fully surrendered followers of Christ who are willing to go anywhere He leads. We must teach them to be missionaries who confront lost persons wherever they go. We must go to the world with what we have, for as long as necessary, taking every risk required to preach the gospel of the kingdom so that every person on earth might hear the good news of salvation.

The Great Commission requires evangelism be the church's and believer's first priority. Following in importance is discipleship, which leads persons to follow Christ completely in everything they do. The power and value of a transformed, authentic spiritual life is immeasurable. The only adequate paradigm for ministry is one that views the present age in terms of the coming kingdom of God.

The present growth and future consummation of the kingdom of God means:

- God is always preparing the world to receive Christ.
- God is always saving persons from their sins and separation from Him.
- God is sending believers on mission with Him to spread the gospel around the world.

Each statement above is not simply an invitation to join God, but a command and a commission to be fulfilled and obeyed by every believer and every church. To fulfill this command, we need prophets, teachers, and resources such as training literature and Bible studies to interpret present world events and cultural realities in the light of God's purposes. We need instruction, exhortation, and motivation to help us focus on the world, the gospel, and our churches' ministries.

It is the very nature of the gospel to confront persons with a message and a way of thinking which is totally foreign and unacceptable to them. Persons without Christ have many reasons and excuses for their problems, not the least of which are pride and self-sufficiency. Persons outside of Christ know something is wrong or missing from their lives, but they do not recognize that the problem comes from within. Jesus Christ invaded our world in the incarnation, revealed sin as evil and separation from God, and placed the responsibility on each individual.

It is the responsibility of every church to take the gospel to every possible person regardless of the response they might receive.

When we bear the gospel to our neighbors and to persons around the world, we will experience the same initial response as Jesus, Peter, Steven, Paul, and countless other persons throughout the centuries. "We preach Christ crucified, to Jews a stumbling block, and to Gentiles foolishness, but to those who are the called ... Christ the power of God and the wisdom of God" (1 Cor. 1:23-24).

When a church commits itself to the biblical functions of evangelism, discipleship, fellowship, ministry, and worship, it will not only see growth numerically, spiritually, and in ministry, but also in missions giving, going, and results.

It is God who sends us and God alone who saves those who hear the gospel from us. God is working to redeem all people, and He has chosen us to do His work in this present age.

The Christian's mission does not develop out of the world's culture, but out of the kingdom of God. Believers and their churches are agencies which together create a missions force without regard to race, gender, nationalities, age, lack of resources, training, or faithlessness. This mission is based on a divine purpose fulfilled by the Father in Christ through the power of the Holy Spirit in the lives of God's people. By God's grace, we are permitted to be God's instruments for this kingdom purpose. We have no greater privilege.

Rewind. Mark the following statements T (true) or F (false).

___ *The Great Commission requires evangelism as the first priority of every believer.*

___ *The nature of the gospel means the message of the gospel will be confrontational.*

___ *Christian mission arises primarily from the needs of the world.*

The first two statements in the **"Rewind"** activity are true, but the last statement is false. While we need to be aware of the needs of people, our mission has the purpose of God as its source.

What are your feelings about the Great Commission? Do you think your church is committed to spreading the gospel around the world? Have you done everything God has asked you to do thus far in your life to join Him as He reaches across the world with the gospel? Are you willing for the Lord to do anything in your life He desires in order for the kingdom of God to advance on earth at this time?

A properly organized and functioning church will experience the joy of seeing missions grow and advance. As a church joins God to establish the kingdom of God around the world, it develops a heartbeat for missions which urges every believer to be a missionary evangelizing the world for Christ.

Missions and Individual Responsibility for Kingdom Growth

The kingdom of God is universal and eternal. The kingdom is a larger reality than the church, but it contains the church. The kingdom, however, is expanded through the lives of individual believers and not just through agencies and institutions. Jesus Christ did not commission local churches and denominations to take the gospel to the entire world; He commissioned persons. God redeems the world one person at a time, and He sends persons on mission with Him the same way. Local churches must focus and organize themselves to extend the kingdom of God through their members. Do not be misled into believing it is the mission organizations' responsibility to do missions. God does not call organizations and institutions to salvation, He calls individuals. He does not send agencies around the world, He sends people like you and me. Building and expanding the kingdom of God is a direct responsibility of individual believers whose hearts and lives are in keeping with the Father's purposes.

Rewind. Circle the word which makes each sentence a true statement about our personal responsibility for the mission of the kingdom of God.

1. Jesus commissioned (individuals, churches) to take the gospel to the world.

2. Jesus calls (individuals, denominations) to missionary advance around the world.

3. Jesus challenges (individuals, organizations) to show His love and make disciples.

"For it [the kingdom of God] is just like a man about to go on a journey, who called his own slaves, and entrusted his possessions to them."

Matthew 25:14

In each of the statements in the *"Rewind"* activity, the word *individuals* makes the statement true. There is always danger in allowing organizations and agencies to dominate kingdom work and set mission strategies for the people of God. No matter how well intentioned and effective these entities seem to be, nothing is more important than individual responsibility in missions. Some believe that God calls people to missions through the church; therefore, a church or denominational agency must recognize and send individuals on mission with God. This is especially applicable when a person feels called to missions overseas. Denominational agencies and boards are important, but regardless of how a church or denomination chooses to help persons who make commitments to serve God, only God sends persons.

Denominational agencies and boards exist to help believers build the kingdom of God, but God has many means and methods to accomplish His redemptive purposes.

Strategies and plans must always be developed in response to what we see God doing. The kingdom of God has suffered throughout Christian history when attempts to carry out the Great Commission were controlled by ecclesiasticism and the involvement of God's people was replaced by only professional clergy. Often this left individual believers out of kingdom service because "professional" ministers determined the scope and work of kingdom ministries.

Another problem in carrying out kingdom work is an unhealthy emphasis on religious dogma. Certainly Bible-based doctrine is essential in our churches, but not to the exclusion of an understanding of the kingdom of God by the people of God. Although doctrine and theology are important, if doctrinal debates divide Christians, they can result in a loss of focus by believers on the Great Commission. There are few people today who can adequately and biblically define the kingdom of God and then accept it as the fundamental reality in our world which moves and shapes history according to God's plan. God is at work in, through, and around us establishing His kingdom. Doctrine is important in our churches, but God's mission for us is the priority.

Another historic tendency in churches which destroys individual responsibility in kingdom work is formalism or ritualizing God's work in a believer's life. This often prevents the Holy Spirit from expressing Himself in the lives of believers and communicating God's will to them for their lives. Formalism is an attempt to control the things of God and the activity of God in our lives. Believers have free and equal access to God through Christ, and His communication to them is vital for service in the kingdom.

The kingdom of God must control and direct our thinking, our prayerlife, and our work with God. This is illustrated by the life and testimony of John L. Shuck, the first medical missionary appointed to China. His commitment to Christ was described by Bill Wallace one hundred years later as follows:

> "I am especially happy to go to China this year, for it is exactly one hundred years ago this month, September 1835, that John Lewis Shuck and Henrietta Hall Shuck set sail for China to be the first Southern Baptist foreign missionaries in China. At a certain service, when an offering was asked for foreign missions, a young man sitting in the rear of the church secured a piece of paper

114

and wrote something on it and dropped it in the collection plate. Later when the gold and silver was being counted, the note was found and said, 'Myself, John Lewis Shuck.' Of silver and gold he had practically none, but such as he had, he gave."[1]

Dr. Shuck was called by God, responded to God's call, and was appointed and supported by a denominational missions agency just as Paul was sent to the Gentiles by God who then led churches to support him in his work.

How has God has called you to fulfill His purposes in declaring His kingdom? Have you responded in a visible, personal way? The responsibility for kingdom work and for missions rests first and foremost upon the individual Christian.

Rewind. *Match the word on the left with its definition to review problems which undermine personal responsibility for mission advance by individuals.*

Ecclesiasticism   *Unhealthy teaching or focus on particular doctrines as the ultimate purpose of believers in the kingdom.*

Dogmatism   *Ritualizing the work of God in or through a believer's life.*

Formalism   *Replacing individual service by believers with professional ministry by vocational clergy.*

Nothing must be allowed to come between us and the God who saves and sends us.

The words above are important because they reflect a serious misunderstanding of the fact that God works through individuals who love Him to accomplish the work of His kingdom. As it is used here, ecclesiasticism refers to the idea of replacing individual kingdom service with professional ministry. Dogmaticism is an unhealthy focusing on beliefs and doctrines. Formalism tends to ritualize the work of God in a believer's life.

The Role of Kingdom Agencies and Organizations
Although the individual believer bears the weight of responsibility for

kingdom work, kingdom agencies and organizations serve a vital and helpful role. The cooperation of believers and churches to evangelize, make disciples, baptize, and teach is as old as Christianity. The kingdom of God makes this a possibility. The kingdom of God calls persons to ministry. Denominations, organizations and agencies help by providing strategies, methods, funding, and opportunity for those who are called by God to join Him in His work. Such agencies and organizations provide administration, training, and support for persons in kingdom ministry. Churches and kingdom institutions are gathering, training, and sending agencies for believers. When believers join hands, they form small streams of support leading to large and powerful rivers which assist God's people in preaching the gospel throughout the world. Kingdom agencies, then, are servants of God's people, not rulers and directors. They educate in kingdom living and ministry, exhort to fulfill the Great Commission, administrate services and resources as stewards, and lead people to share Christ. But they must not take away from believers their responsibility before God to work in His kingdom.

As individual believers we must come into the presence of the Lord and acknowledge that as sovereign ruler of His kingdom He sends persons to accomplish His purposes.

The Gospel of the Kingdom

It may seem strange to focus our attention on the gospel of Christ at this stage in our study. We have considered the kingdom of God in several aspects, but we will end our discussion with a consideration of the gospel. The gospel is the story of Jesus Christ's coming into the world, inaugurating the kingdom of God, teaching about the kingdom of God, and providing a way into the kingdom of God through His death and resurrection. The gospel is the power of God's salvation to any person who hears and believes it. The gospel introduces lost persons to Jesus Christ. Incredible as it may seem to us, there are people around the world who have never heard of Jesus Christ. The gospel presents His story in time and history and educates people about His claims and great works. But it's more than that. No other historical account possesses transforming power. The power of the gospel comes from the Holy Spirit and brings persons from ignorance to repentance of sins and a saving faith in Christ.

Paul preached that the gospel is the power of God for salvation. It produces faith in the hearer. As Paul wrote in Romans 10:17, "So faith comes from hearing, and hearing by the word of Christ." The Spirit uses the gospel of Christ to bring spiritual understanding and life.

God uses the gospel as His instrument and believers as His

* *God is on mission and calls us to join Him.*
* *God is sovereign, and He does His work as He chooses.*
* *God's ways are perfect and His motives are pure.*
* *God is growing His kingdom which cannot be stopped.*
* *God uses many ways, persons, and methods to accomplish His work.*

vehicles to confront lost persons. No person is saved without hearing the gospel, and no person will hear the gospel unless believers bear personal responsibility to share it.

It is the nature of the gospel to confront persons with their sin and help them to understand that their needs can only be met in a personal relationship with Christ. The gospel assumes there is something lacking in persons and their individual cultures. Through the gospel the Holy Spirit makes them uncomfortable in their sinful lifestyles and convicts them to repent of sins and live in righteousness and holiness. We must come to a point in our lives where our compassion for lost humanity causes us to weep and pray while we are compelled by love to share the gospel of Jesus Christ with all who will hear. This gospel of Christ is powerful enough to bring lost persons to salvation through repentance and faith in Christ.

Our world is in constant transition and crisis. Society's problems are far beyond the reach of our own limited resources. Government, education, science, technology, psychology, and management cannot meet the demands of life. Only God can meet the needs of every individual. This happens when people discover Him in the gospel.

Our world looks to materialism, science, and hedonism for answers, but these avenues guarantee destruction as people and nations run away from God. People are torn by contradictions, broken promises, failed political agendas, false religions, and a secular mind-set which has cultivated a pessimistic and hopeless environment. Pain, fear, and despair run rampant. Nothing is considered sacred or absolute, so to many life is cheap and meaningless.

The good news of Christ breaks into the lives of those ruined by false philosophies, ideologies, and world systems to offer hope, meaning, and purpose. It challenges a person's every thought, every experience, and every resource until that person comes to Christ. The gospel brings the ultimate paradigm shift and points persons away from destruction and misery to life and peace in Christ. It is our kingdom duty to seize every opportunity to share the gospel of the kingdom of God. The method of sharing is our choice as long as we do not change the message and the meaning of the message. The gospel is the world's ultimate resource for hope and meaning.

The Consummation of the Kingdom
When will the Lord Jesus return? The disciples were the first to ask

"The gospel ... is the power of God for salvation to everyone who believes."
Romans 1:16

We must remember that our kingdom responsibility is to share this powerful gospel with every person we can in order to confront them with the power of God that can change their lives.

this question of the Savior before He returned to heaven. It is an important question because it speaks to the time we have left to accomplish our kingdom tasks. It is also important because it affirms the excitement of knowing that one day Jesus Christ will appear, and we shall go with Him to eternity in heaven. His words in John 14:3 comfort us in our most stressful times, "And if I go and prepare a place for you, I will come again, and receive you to Myself; that where I am, there you may be also." To live for Christ on earth and to be with Christ in heaven is sufficient motivation for us as we face life.

However, the question "When?" is not easily answered. Even Jesus deferred to the Father regarding the time of the consummation of the kingdom when He said, "But of that day or hour no one knows, not even the angels in heaven, nor the Son, but the Father alone" (Mark 13:32). For us, then, the kingdom of God is considered in process as history nears a final dramatic climax. The kingdom *was* the center of Jesus' earthly ministry, it *is* the focus of God's activity through Christ on earth today, and one day, when Christ returns, the kingdom *will be* revealed in its completeness.

"When they had come together, they were asking Him, saying, 'Lord is it at this time You are restoring the kingdom to Israel?' "

Acts 1:6

There is a tension between Christ's present rule and His coming reign. The kingdom of God is a historical reality, but how does one reconcile the tension we read in the Bible between the imminent or immediate return of the Lord and the moving of history through predicted events which must take place before the Lord returns? It is not our task in this study to examine the Scripture passages which point to these two truths about the kingdom of God, but each truth is important for our lives and ministries.

The tension exists, in part, because of the difference between prophetic and apocalyptic types of writing in Scripture. The prophets in general concentrated on the kingdom of God and the demands in the world for justice, righteousness, and repentance. They were generally pessimistic toward the world and its systems and concentrated upon God's movement in history to vindicate His holy name and purpose. Apocalyptic writings like those in Daniel and Revelation revealed the kingdom of God as high drama with a focus on the conflict between God and Satan. The kingdom of God was established while earthly kingdoms were destroyed. These writings indicate a future optimism despite catastrophic conflicts which must occur before Christ returns.

Rewind. *Place an "A" by the following words and phrases which describe apocalyptic literature. Place a "P" by the words and phrases which describe prophetic literature.*

____ *Generally pessimistic*
____ *Generally optimistic*
____ *Focus on conflict between good and evil*
____ *Focus on demands for justice and righteousness*
____ *God is moving in history*
____ *God will move in the future*

Let's review the differences between prophetic and apocalyptic material. The prophets were generally pessimistic. Their message focused on justice and righteousness. In spite of their pessimism concerning world systems, they believed that God moves in history. The writers of apocalyptic literature expressed a point of view that was optomistic about the future. They saw the conflict between good and evil, but they believed God would move in future history.

The Bible presents all of these truths. Although they appear to contradict each other, they are essential to understanding the consummation of the kingdom at the end of the age. The kingdom of God was established as God moved through history to complete His redemptive purposes. The time of this kingdom was marked by the coming of Jesus Christ, born to the virgin Mary. His birth, life, ministry, death, resurrection, and ascension are historical events which served to inaugurate the kingdom of God on earth. Just as the kingdom was proclaimed on earth by Jesus, it will be consummated on earth. God will break into history one last dramatic time when Christ returns to earth, and the kingdom will be established. Christ's reign over all things on earth will be visible, and Scripture's proclamation will be reality, "The kingdom of the world has become the kingdom of our Lord, and of His Christ; and He will reign forever and ever" (Rev. 11:15).

At this point, Christians will realize the full meaning of the kingdom of God when we reign on earth with Him. John, in the Book of Revelation, heard the four living creatures and the 24 elders praising Jesus Christ the Lamb of God singing a "new song" saying:

> *"Worthy art Thou to take the book, and to break its seals;*
> *for Thou wast slain, and didst purchase for God with Thy*

The kingdom of God was the center of Jesus' ministry on earth. It represented the rule of God coming through Him. It meant that God is on mission to bring people from the domain of darkness and sin to the kingdom of light.

119

blood men from every tribe and tongue and people and nation. And Thou has made them to be a kingdom and priests to our God; and they will reign upon the earth" (Rev. 5:9-10).

When Christ comes to reign on earth we will join Him, and all the world will know that He is indeed King of kings and Lord of lords. What does this mean for us today? Consider the following biblical truths concerning the kingdom of God at the return of Christ:

- God acts in history within the lives of His people, but also outside their lives.
- Evil is real, personal, and destructive and can be overcome only by God's direct intervention.
- God reaps total victory over Satan, sin, and evil in the person and work of Christ. If this is not true, then the kingdom of God is an empty dream.
- The kingdom of God exists only through God's activity.
- The kingdom will be a total redemption of men and nature in order to provide a perfect setting for the people of God.

Since the kingdom is the moving force of history, it must also be the culmination of history.

Jesus gave many signs of His second coming but none so dramatic as in Matthew.

"But immediately after the tribulation of those days the sun will be darkened, and the moon will not give its light, and the stars will fall from the sky, and the powers of the heavens will be shaken, and then the sign of the Son of Man will appear in the sky, and then all the tribes of the earth will mourn, and they will see the Son of Man coming on the clouds of the sky with power and great glory. And He will send forth His angels with a great trumpet and they will gather together His elect from the four winds, from one end of the sky to the other" (Matt. 24:29).

Before the return of Christ the natural order will experience extreme chaos, violence, and wars as people and nations are overcome by evil. Read Paul's description of the last days.

"Men will be lovers of self, lovers of money, boastful, arrogant, revilers, disobedient to parents, ungrateful,

unholy, unloving, irreconcilable, malicious gossips, without self-control, brutal, haters of good, treacherous, reckless, conceited, lovers of pleasure rather than lovers of God" (2 Tim. 3:2-4).

Even though these events will be difficult for all persons on earth, believers will recognize there are signs that Jesus Christ will soon return to the earth to reign. As believers who are aware of history's movement, we expect the sudden return of Christ and must live in readiness and hope. We cannot live as persons uninformed of Jesus' return. A watchful and hopeful eye keeps us from being absorbed into the decadence of our culture. It also gives us something to live for and something to leave for future generations if His return is beyond our own lives.

We must guard our hearts and lives in Christ in order to be ready for the hour when He returns.

Stop and Think! *In a deteriorating culture, what is the basis of your hope for the future?*

Until we begin our reign with Christ in the consummated kingdom of God, we must pray, work, go, and teach all nations. What a glorious hour when we reach the end of our labors and meet the Lord and the saints in the kingdom. Personally, I want to arrive at that time in my life completely expended for Christ and for His kingdom. I do not want to go to the kingdom of God having failed to complete any task. Nothing is more important and gives more meaning to life than to be part of His Kingdom.

We may not be able to understand all the mysteries and meaning of the kingdom of God; but we can act upon what we do know.

Have you ever walked by a construction site and looked through one of the peep holes to get a view of the work that is going on? If you tried to describe what you were seeing to another person you might mention some of the equipment, such as cranes and trucks. You might identify some of the various workmen at the site, such as steel workers or electricians. Then you might try to describe what the structure looks like. But unless the person looked through the peephole himself, he would not fully understand what you tried to describe. Of course, if you returned a week later your description would change because the work would be further along.

In our study we have tried to describe many biblical truths about the kingdom; but to truly understand it, you must look at it and experience it for yourself. Of course, just as the building in the story grows to completion, each of us must realize that the kingdom is a growing reality that is moving toward complete fulfillment.

By His power we can adjust our lives to conform to Christ and join the Father in His kingdom work. With your present understanding of the kingdom, will you surrender your life to the purposes of God without regard to self-interests? Will you follow Christ wherever He leads on earth knowing that you are part of the kingdom of God? Will you devote your thoughts and actions to the kingdom of God? Will you support and love the kingdom as you love Jesus Christ your Lord? May Christ find each of us faithful, working, loving, and waiting when He returns. Maranatha! Come, Lord Jesus.

Stop and Think! *As you consider the questions at the conclusion of this study, prayerfully consider renewing your commitment to Jesus Christ and work in the kingdom of God by signing this Kingdom Covenant.*

> *It is worthwhile for believers to seek first the kingdom of God and the righteousness He provides in Christ. It is worth the struggles, the tribulation, the temptations, the sorrows, and the pain to press forward to Christ's calling—the high calling to salvation and eternal life in the kingdom of God.*

KINGDOM COVENANT

I surrender the rest of my life, without reservation, to God's purposes for me in His kingdom.

I will follow God's plan for my life, wherever He leads, and willingly serve Him in His kingdom.

I will serve the kingdom of God with humility, whatever station I am assigned.

I will be found faithful through God's grace and strength, working, loving, and waiting when the kingdom is consummated.

Signed _____

---

¹Jesse Fletcher, *Bill Wallace of China* (Nashville: Broadman & Holman, 1996), 234.

Concordance
New Testament References to the Kingdom

Matthew 3:2

Matthew 4:17

Matthew 4:23

Matthew 5:3

Matthew 5:10

Matthew 5:19

Matthew 5:20

Matthew 6:10

Matthew 6:13

Matthew 6:33

Matthew 7:21

Matthew 8:11

Matthew 8:12

Matthew 9:35

Matthew 10:7

Matthew 11:11

Matthew 11:12

Matthew 12:25

Matthew 12:26

Matthew 12:28

Matthew 13:11

Matthew 13:19

Matthew 13:24

Matthew 13:31

Matthew 13:33

Matthew 13:38

Matthew 13:41

Matthew 13:43

Matthew 13:44

Matthew 13:45

Matthew 13:47

Matthew 13:52

Matthew 16:19

Matthew 16:28

Matthew 18:1

Matthew 18:3

Matthew 18:4

Matthew 18:23

Matthew 19:12

Matthew 19:14

Matthew 19:23

Matthew 19:24

Matthew 20:1

Matthew 20:21

Matthew 21:31

Matthew 21:43

Matthew 22:2

Matthew 23:13

Matthew 24:7

Matthew 24:14

Matthew 25:1

Matthew 25:14

Matthew 25:34

Matthew 26:29

Mark 1:14

Mark 1:15

Mark 3:24

Mark 4:11

Mark 4:26

Mark 4:30

Mark 6:23

Mark 9:1

Mark 9:47

Mark 10:14

Mark 10:15

Mark 10:23

Mark 10:24

Mark 10:25

Mark 11:10

Mark 12:34

Mark 13:8

Mark 14:25

Mark 15:43

Luke 1:33

Luke 4:43

Luke 23:42

Luke 6:20

Luke 23:51

Luke 7:28

John 3:3

Luke 8:1

John 3:5

Luke 8:10

John 18:36

Luke 9:2

Acts 1:3

Luke 9:11

Acts 1:6

Luke 9:27

Acts 8:12

Luke 9:60

Acts 14:22

Luke 9:62

Acts 19:8

Luke 10:9

Acts 20:25

Luke 10:11

Acts 28:23

Luke 11:2

Acts 28:31

Luke 11:17

Romans 14:17

Luke 11:18

1 Corinthians 4:20

Luke 11:20

1 Corinthians 6:9

Luke 12:31

1 Corinthians 6:10

Luke 12:32

1 Corinthians 15:24

Luke 13:18

1 Corinthians 15:50

Luke 13:20

Galatians 5:21

Luke 13:28

Ephesians 5:5

Luke 13:29

Colossians 1:13

Luke 14:15

Colossians 4:11

Luke 16:16

1 Thessalonians 2:12

Luke 17:20

2 Thessalonians 1:5

Luke 17:21

2 Thessalonians 4:1

Luke 18:16

2 Thessalonians 4:18

Luke 18:17

Hebrews 1:8

Luke 18:24

Hebrews 12:28

Luke 18:25

James 2:5

Luke 18:29

2 Peter 1:11

Luke 19:11

Revelation 1:6

Luke 19:12

Revelation 1:9

Luke 19:15

Revelation 5:10

Luke 21:10

Revelation 11:15

Luke 21:31

Revelation 12:10

Luke 22:16

Revelation 16:10

Luke 22:18

Revelation 17:12

Luke 22:29

Revelation 17:17

Luke 22:30

CHRISTIAN GROWTH STUDY PLAN

Preparing Christians to Serve

In the **Christian Growth Study Plan (formerly Church Study Course),** this book *Thine Is the Kingdom: The Reign of God in Today's World is a* resource for course credit in the subject area Baptist Doctrine of the Christian Growth category of diploma plans. To receive credit, read the book, complete the learning activities, show your work to your pastor, a staff member or church leader, then complete the information on the next page. The form may be duplicated. Send the completed page to:

Christian Growth Study Plan
127 Ninth Avenue, North, MSN 117
Nashville, TN 37234-0117
FAX: (615)251-5067

For information about the Christian Growth Study Plan, refer to the current Christian Growth Study Plan Catalog. Your church office may have a copy. If not, request a free copy from the Christian Growth Study Plan office (615/251-2525).

Thine is the Kingdom

COURSE NUMBER: CG- 0368

PARTICIPANT INFORMATION

Social Security Number | Personal CGSP Number* | Date of Birth

Name (First, MI, Last)
☐ Mr. ☐ Miss
☐ Mrs. ☐

Home Phone

Address (Street, Route, or P.O. Box) | City, State | Zip Code

CHURCH INFORMATION

Church Name

Address (Street, Route, or P.O. Box) | City, State | Zip Code

CHANGE REQUEST ONLY

☐ Former Name

☐ Former Address | City, State | Zip Code

☐ Former Church | City, State | Zip Code

Signature of Pastor, Conference Leader, or Other Church Leader | Date

*New participants are requested but not required to give SS# and date of birth. Existing participants, please give CGSP# when using SS# for the first time.

Thereafter, only one ID# is required. *Mail To:* Christian Growth Study Plan, 127 Ninth Ave., North, MSN 117, Nashville, TN 37234-0117. Fax: (615)251-5067